M000315320

THE

GAME

CHANGER

Winning Strategies to Obtain Veterans' Disability, Social Security, and Appeals

— THE —
GAME
CHANGER

Winning Strategies to Obtain Veterans' Disability, Social Security, and Appeals

Jimmy Cave

gatekeeper press

Columbus, Ohio

The Game Changer: Winning Strategies to Obtain Veterans' Disability, Social Security, and Appeals

Resources for Veterans and Family Series – Book 1

Published by Gatekeeper Press
2167 Stringtown Rd, Suite 109
Columbus, OH 43123-2989
www.GatekeeperPress.com

Library of Congress Control Number: 2020945590

ISBN (hardcover): 9781662904479
ISBN (paperback): 9781662904486
eISBN: 9781662904493

Contents

Acknowledgments x

Thank you for your service xii

Disclaimer xiii

Introduction xiv

Who is considered a veteran? 1

Health care at VA medical center 2

Vet centers 4

Definition of a disability 5

Five ways to be approved for disability 6

Most common disabilities 9

Body systems that are rated for disability 14

VA rating chart and symptoms 15

Low-value claims vs High-value claims 16

Personality disorder 19

Federal Veterans' Laws, Rules and Regulations 20

eBenefits: https://www.eBenefits.va.gov 22

Forms and documents required in veteran's claim:
VSO representatives 24

    VA form 21-686c - declaration of status of dependent 25

    DD 214 – certificate of release or discharge from active duty 26

    VA form 21-526EZ - application for disability compensation 27

Write the correct word of conditions you're claiming for disability . . 29

VA medical records - https://myhealth.va.gov 34

How to request medical records 35

How to request military service records 37

Tricare online 38

Physical therapy. 40

Prosthetic and sensory aids. 41

Emergency room. 42

Nexus letter from doctor 44

50/50 rule 49

Purpose of an independent medical opinion/nexus letter 51

Published medical reports in an independent medical opinion 53

DBQ form from doctor 54

Disability symptoms and diagnosis. 56

C&P examination or QTC exam 58

Proving severity of conditions. 60

Buddy letters/lay evidence. 61

Confirmed stressor letter. 62

How to request a DD-214 upgrade from dishonorable to
honorable discharge 63

Recently discharged veterans 65

Different types of VA claims. 66

The best time to apply for VA disability 68

VA claims effective date. 70

Track status of VA claims by calling VA at 1-800-827-1000. 72

How to apply for an increase in disability ratings 73

Total disability based on individual unemployability (TDIU) = IU . .76

What to do if the regional office denies your TDIU claim. 83

VA TDIU unemployability (TDIU) and social security benefits. 85

VA compensation & pension exams or QTC exams 88

How to get social security as a private citizen 91

Social security survivor beneficiaries 96

VA pension and fiduciary services. 97

Caregiver program 100

Proposal to reduce rating/rating reduction. 102

Situations in which the VA can reduce a veteran's rating 104
Why veterans are denied benefits. 105
Purpose of VA routine C&P or QTC exams 107
VA rating protections 108
Veteran's disability claims neglect 110
Clear and unmistakable error claim (CUE) 113
VA regulation definition of a clear unmistakable error (CUE) 114
VA patient advocacy 117
You win when you appeal to the Board of Veterans' Appeals (BVA) 118
Veterans' options when denied a claim from the regional office. . . . 119
Benefits of hiring an attorney to file appeals 124
Post-traumatic stress disorder (PTSD) rating scale 128
Mental health. 130
Well-grounded claim law. 135
How to apply for post-traumatic stress disorder (PTSD) 137
Veterans and military crisis line. 138
Special monthly compensation. 139
Obstructive sleep apnea 141
VA rating for sleep apnea. 146
Migraine headaches 147
Hypertension or high blood pressure 148
Definition of permanent disability (P&T). 150
Chapter 35 - Dependents' educational assistance 152
ChampVA dependents healthcare 153
Humana care 154
VA dental treatment 155
Blind rehabilitation services 156
Benefits based on a veteran's seriously disabled child 157
Specially adapted housing/special home adaptation 158
VetSuccess 159

Co-payments 160
Reimbursement for travel mileage 161
Clothing allowance 162
Disabled veterans' student loan forgiveness program 163
Automobile grant 164
Disabled veterans' plate 165
Property tax and VA funding fees exempted 166
Free or reduced state park annual membership 167
State benefits 168
Commissary and exchange privileges 169
Free parking at airport and cruise terminals 170
Defense finance & accounting center 171
VA life insurance 172
Burial and memorial service 173
Conclusion 175
VA phone numbers 177
VA web sites 178
About the author 179

The just shall live by faith

"For I know the **plans** that I have for you, says the Lord, thoughts of **peace** and not of evil, to give you a **future** and a **hope**. Then you will **call upon me** and go and **pray** to me, and I **will listen to your prayers**. And you will **read God's word** and **find me**, when you **search** for me with **all your heart**."
-Jeremiah 29:11-13

"Then the Lord answered me and said: '**Write** the **vision** and **make** it **plain** on tablets, that he may run who **reads it**. For the **vision** is yet for the **appointed time**; but at the end **it will not lie**. But the **righteous** shall **live** by **faith**.'"
Habakkuk 2:2-4

"**Faith** is the substance of **things hoped for**, the **evidence** of **things not seen**."
-Hebrews 11:1

"Jesus said to him, "If you can **believe**, **all** things are **possible** to him who believes. Immediately the father of child cried out in tears, 'Lord, help my **unbelief**.'"
-Mark 9:23-24

"So Jesus answered and said to them, '**have faith in God**. For assuredly, I say to you, whoever says to this mountain, be removed and be cast into the sea, and **does not doubt in his heart**, **but believes** that those **things he says will be done**, he will have **whatever he says**. Therefore I say to you, whatever things you **ask** when you **pray**, **believe** that you **receive** them, and you will **have them**.'"
-Mark 11:22-24

Acknowledgments

I would like to give thanks to my savior, Jesus Christ, God, and the holy spirit that lives in me for giving me vision, knowledge, wisdom, and understanding to write this book. Also thanks to my parents and everyone who contributed to my success in life. It has been a struggle to fight the VA (the Department of Veteran Affairs) for hard-earned benefits that the government promised me when I raised my right hand and gave a life of service to this country.

Americans must understand that freedom is not free. I am the first one to admit there were times in my life when I felt like throwing in the towel and giving up. I was a homeless veteran returning from war in Iraq, nowhere to lay my head, no family to greet me when I got off the plane. The VA rejected me from entering their homeless shelter when I needed it the most. I was at my lowest point in life.

But I made it through to become an author to tell my story. In fact, everyone has a story to tell. The graveyards are full of untold stories and full of dreams not fulfilled. The bible says "God has given each one a measure of faith or gift." -Romans 12:3. Everyone has a gift, even with the least amount of effort, to uplift and build people up. That's the purpose of God's gift to us. Not self-gratification, but encouraging and loving one another, because you never know if a person is going through difficult times or even thinking about suicide. A kind word and a smile could be the game changer in a person's life.

This book is a piece of my legacy. I'm dedicating this work to my son to show him if I can overcome the odds to become a great author, and hopefully one day become a bestselling author, and inspire others, he certainly can too. And I am leaving another legacy behind: helping veterans and their family members obtain well-earned benefits.

As a veteran, I fought the VA regional office for 21 years. I feel I have a lot of knowledge to offer in this book with my experience as a former employer at the vet center, Veterans Benefits Administration, and the

VA Medical Center. God placed it on my heart to write on paper and make it plain for veterans and their family members to understand the process of getting VA benefits. Never give up, keep the faith, study the rules regarding the claims you're seeking, and keep going to the doctor because God has the final word.

"If God is for us, who can be against us? Who shall bring a charge against God's elect? It is God who justifies. It is Christ who died, and furthermore is also risen, who is even sitting at the right hand of God, who makes intercession for us. Who shall separate us from the love of Christ? Shall tribulation, or distress, or persecution, or famine, or nakedness, or peril, or sword? Yet in all these things we are more than conquerors through Christ who loved us." – Romans 8:31-38

Thank you for your service

I would like to give special thanks to my publisher for providing insights and suggestions and checking for accuracy.

I would also like to dedicate this book to all military members, active duty members, veterans, and their loved ones and thank them for their sacrifice to our country.

Personal Request

I am asking that if you feel you enjoyed this book and feel it has been beneficial to you in learning about The Game Changer: How To Obtain Veterans' Disability, Social Security, And Appeals, please write a POSITIVE REVIEW so that other people might be convinced that they too, can obtain hard earned VA Benefits.

Disclaimer

Please be aware that VA laws and regulations are constantly changing even as I write this book! Take the resources that I provide and do your own research. I am not an accredited agent, VSO, attorney, or doctor. I am not affiliated with the VA in any way. It is best you do your own research and seek an attorney for legal advice and your doctor regarding medical diagnosis and/or treatments. This book is for educational purposes only and should not be substituted for the medical advice from a doctor or healthcare provider or legal advice of a VA accredited attorney.

Introduction

The purpose of this book is to educate military members who are separating or retiring, active duty members, veterans, and their loved ones on the process of how to file VA claims, VA appeals, and apply for social security benefits. Also, what key medical evidence is needed to submit to your private doctors, the VA regional office, employer human resources, and social security. It is important to learn the VA and social security laws, rules, and regulations for yourself because navigating both agencies can be complicated. I will also explain how you can get your student loans discharged or wiped away.

I had the honor and privilege to work at the vet center, the Veterans Benefits Administration (VBA), and the VA hospital as an Iraq combat veteran. I feel my experience and education will be a great asset to all veterans and their family members seeking benefits from the VA and social security. Looking back on my career, I know it was my calling to serve and to write this book to show veterans and family members my appreciation and gratitude for their fighting to protect and preserve our great nation. Thank you for your service.

As a former employee at the Veterans Benefits Administration, I witnessed how the VBA gave veterans the "run around" making it difficult for veterans to get the benefits they deserve. I have firsthand knowledge of how veterans are mistreated, including myself, waiting years to be eventually denied benefits. I saw how veterans service officers denied veterans just to relieve the workload off their desks. It took me 21 years of fighting the VA regional office tooth and nail to get permanent and total status after appealing denied claims to a judge in Washington, D.C. several times.

Many veterans get tired of fighting the VA and give up, while other veterans die waiting to see if they were approved. Recently, the VA added more complex forms for veterans to complete. After learning the rules and regulations, I witnessed how the VA made it difficult for me as a combat veteran to obtain the benefits that I sacrificed my life for, for this great country of ours to enjoy freedom and liberty! And all we as veterans are requesting is for America to keep its promise to return its obligations to care for us veterans. President Lincoln's promise was to "care for him who shall have borne the battle, and for his widow, and his orphan."

My aim is to educate veterans and their family members on the process of obtaining veterans benefits, including a step-by-step guide to establishing a well-grounded claim and how to obtain social security benefits. According to a government accountability office report in 2017, the VA denied more than 80% of veterans' claims for benefits for Gulf War illnesses - an approval rating three times lower than any other type of claim. A lot of times, claims are denied simply because veterans do not understand the rules and regulations written by Congress, which lists what documents to submit and the process of becoming a disabled veteran.

My goal for this book is to explain:

1. How veterans and civilians must take ownership of their VA claims, social security, and appeals.
2. How to successfully navigate the VA and social security system for disability benefits and appeals.
3. How to apply for VA disability, VA pension, and social security.
4. How five-star medical evidence in medical records helps win disability claims and appeals.
5. How getting independent medical opinions (nexus letters) and diagnoses from private doctors for VA claims can be a game changer for veterans.
6. How to keep your claim from getting lost or sitting on the shelf.
7. How to speed up the process of disability claims for VA benefits and social security.

Who is considered a veteran?

Title 38 of the code of federal regulations defines a veteran as "a person who served in the active military, naval, or air service and who was discharged or released under conditions other than dishonorable." A person cannot be a veteran if they received dishonorable discharge!

Another example of a veteran would be someone who has served in various military academies or has attendance in a military preparatory school. When a person enters into the service and injures themselves while in basic training, he/she receives a service-connected disability rating from the VA. Then they would be considered a veteran no matter how many days they served in the United States military. To qualify for VA disability compensation or VA medical care, only one day of active duty is required.

Members of the National Guard and Reserves may be considered veterans if they were deployed under title 10 (federal orders) and have completed that deployment and were issued a DD-214 (discharge) under honorable conditions. The veteran must have served 180 days. You do not have to be a combat veteran to receive VA disability. In fact, a veteran can be service-connected for almost any injury that occurred while in the military, no matter the location as long as the military service member was on active duty and provides a copy of their DD-214 and active duty orders.

Health care at VA medical center

The VA medical center offers a variety of health care services to veterans who are enrolled or registered. After a veteran has enrolled, the eligibility office will assign him/her to a primary care doctor near the veteran's home of residence. Be advised that if you stop visiting the VA hospital after two years (no show), you will no longer be eligible for services at the VA hospital. You will have the problem of lack of medical evidence when it comes time to file for disability. So do not hurt yourself because you see no need to go to the doctor! Many times, veterans are denied for disability due to lack of medical evidence in their medical records.

Services provided at the VA hospital include:

- Immunization
- Physical examinations
- Health-care assessments
- Screening test
- Emergency care in VA facilities
- Surgical care (including reconstructive/plastic surgery assessment of disease or trauma)
- Chiropractic care
- Medications
- Bereavement counseling
- Readjustment counseling
- Specialized health care for female veterans
- Homeless veteran programs
- Alcohol and drug dependency treatment
- Treatment related to military sexual trauma (MST)
- Individual and group counseling for mental health conditions
- Medical evaluation for disorders related to Gulf War services or environmental hazards

- Domiciliary, nursing home, and community-based residential care
- Hospital, outpatient medical, dental, pharmacy, and prosthetic services

Veterans who are eligible to receive healthcare treatment at the VA medical center must enroll or register. Veteran can contact the health benefits call center at 877-222-8387 or visit their nearest VA medical center to register for medical care. You can also log on to the VA health care eligibility website: **http://www.va.gov/healtheligibility**. You must complete VA form 10-EZ application for health benefits and turn it in to the VA hospital eligibility department in person or by mailing the completed application to the nearest health eligibility center in your district. For southeast:

Health Eligibility Center
2957 Clairmont Road NE, Suite 200
Atlanta, Georgia 30329-1647

Vet centers

Vet centers offer combat veterans counseling through a nationwide community-based program. Counselors offer individual, group, and family readjustment counseling to help you with the transition to civilian life, treat post-traumatic stress disorder (PTSD), or help you with any other military-related issues. Other vet centers include: outreach, education, veteran services, homes for homeless veterans, medical referral, employment, and VA benefit referral. There are over 300 vet centers nationwide that offer these services to veterans, active duty, guard, reservist, and their family. You can reach the vet center locator by calling 877-927-8387.

Definition of a disability

According to the American Disabilities Act (ADA), a disability is "a physical or mental impairment that substantially limits one or more of the major life activities of such individual; a record of such impairment; or being regarded as having such an impairment."

Veterans should do their own research before applying for VA disability or social security disability. The VA's website: **benefits.va.gov** includes a wide variety of information where you can learn the rating scale for each disability and the symptoms of different disabilities.

There are several factors the VA looks for in a veteran's c-file to determine if they qualify for disability. This includes: frequency or how often the veteran visits the doctor or emergency room, severity or pain level, and duration or how long the pain lasts.

There are five types of disability impairments: mobility, cognitive, visual, hearing, and speech. Veterans who obtain an injury or illness while on active duty in service qualify to apply for disability benefits. This is called "service-connected" (SC) disability. The second way a veteran can get a service-connected disability from the VA is when a veteran had a condition before entering the military and while on active duty, the military aggravated or made the condition worse. But the Veterans Benefits Administration only focuses on the first, whether or not your injury occurred while on active duty. In both cases, the veteran must have medical records to prove he or she had an illness before entering service and medical records while on active duty that include a doctor's diagnosis. Also, a veteran must have been discharged under 'other than dishonorable' conditions to qualify for service-connected disability benefits.

Five ways to be approved for disability

1. **Pre-service aggravation** - The veteran had a condition before entering the military and while in the military, the military service aggravated it. It must be documented by doctors and noted in military entrance papers as evidence the military was aware of the condition and accepted the veteran into the military with the condition. It is to the veteran's advantage to save medical reports and exams showing you had a diagnosis and medical treatment before entering service to prove to the VA that the condition has gotten worse since entering the military. You must have "ongoing treatment" for the same condition while in the military and after military service to qualify for disability.

2. **Direct service connection** – The veteran was injured, treated, diagnosed, or complained about a condition while on active duty service or deployed from reserve unit. Most ratings are granted from this category. VA will not consider a veteran for disability from all five categories, but make decisions based on one of the five ways to qualify for disability. The veteran must tell the full truth. So go on sick call and see a doctor every time you are in pain because your body will get old and one day you will exit the military with lifelong disabilities that you will seek compensation for from the VA. So plan ahead; you will not be young forever!

3. **Secondary service connection** – The veteran must already have a service-connected condition that has caused another condition that can be service connected. An example would be low back pain that caused another condition like sciatica nerve pain. The sciatica nerve pain causes pain in the nerves that run from the lower back down the back of the legs to the bottom of the feet.

In most cases, the secondary condition's rating exceeds the original service-connected disability. A secondary service connection is most helpful when a veteran is at 90% and is seeking 100% permanent & total (P&T). The VA math system is complicated and technically you need another 50% rating to get from 90% to 100% P&T. Veterans miss out on the secondary claims, which can be a game changer.

4. **Increase in a service-connected condition** – The veteran is already service-connected for a condition but feels the condition has gotten worse. The VA automatically conducts C&P exams every three years until the veteran has "permanent and total" status. The veteran will have to get an updated nexus letter from a doctor stating conditions have gotten worse.

   There are two ways to get an increased service-connected condition. The first way is completing 526-EZ. The second way is to appeal every decision from the regional office, including denial letters, by requesting your doctor type a nexus letter stating conditions have gotten worse since your last C&P exam. Submit x-rays, exams, and reports. I have found that it is best to have a private doctor for every VA doctor you see because the private doctor works in your best interest! You must have a plan in place to challenge the regional office and challenge the VA doctors because they work at the same VA.

5. **Presumptive service connection**:
   a. **Agent Orange presumptive** – The veteran had to have been deployed in Thailand during a specific time or specific job where they sprayed Agent Orange.
   b. **Gulf War presumptive** – The VA presumes that unexplained symptoms are related to Gulf War service if a veteran has experienced them for six months or more. Therefore, by law a veteran who meets certain criteria does not have to prove a relation between their illness and military service. A nexus letter is not required from a private doctor but helps your case! Conditions include: abnormal weight loss,

cardiovascular disease, muscle and joint pain, headache, menstrual disorders, neurological and psychological problems, and skin conditions.

c. **Camp Lejeune presumptive** – Veterans who served at Marine Corps Base Camp Lejeune or Marine Corps Air Station New River in North Carolina from August 1953 to December 1987 may have had contact with contaminants in the drinking water. The veteran must also be diagnosed with one of the following conditions listed: Parkinson's disease, adult leukemia, bladder cancer, liver cancer, multiple myeloma.

d. **One year presumptive** – The veteran must see a VA doctor, preferably a private doctor, ASAP after returning home from deployment while they are still on active duty orders. Veterans must be diagnosed and receive "ongoing treatment" within one year after release from active duty. Veterans also diagnosed with chronic diseases (such as arthritis, diabetes, or hypertension) are encouraged to **apply for disability compensation ASAP after discharge from active duty, within one year, and continue to get ongoing treatment after discharge from the military.** This makes it easier to prove you have a medical condition based on VA regulation. This was another game changer for me. I read and studied the laws many years ago before being deployed to Iraq and the knowledge paid off.

Most common disabilities

The list of VA disability claims that most veterans get approved for include the following:

1. **Bilateral hearing loss**

   Bilateral hearing loss affects both in combat and non-combat veterans. If a veteran's occupation involved working around aircraft all day, they would likely be exposed to loud noises, which may result in a heightened risk of hearing loss later in life. The veteran then would be assigned 10% service-connected rating for hearing loss in both ears, which is considered two disabilities because it is "bilateral." The rating is based on two auditory tests: speech discrimination (assesses how well an individual understands words) and the second auditory test (tests the softest sound audible to an individual at least 50 percent of the time).

2. **Tinnitus**

   Tinnitus is the second most commonly claimed condition for VA disability benefits. This condition is usually described as "ringing in the ears," but it occurs when no external sound is present. (I experience this a lot especially when it is quiet around the home. It is very annoying. To reduce the loud ringing in the ears, I turn the tv sound up or listen to music.) You do not need a specific diagnosis of tinnitus to be granted service connection. Instead, you can provide a subjective report of your symptomatology and that should be enough to show the VBA that you meet the rating criteria. The highest rating for tinnitus is 10%, but you can later apply for a secondary claim in which the tinnitus has caused a mental health disability such as anxiety or depression or migraine headaches. You can then claim 70% mental health disability secondary to tinnitus or

50% migraine headache secondary to tinnitus. There you see the secondary claims are rated higher than the original claim for tinnitus, which is only 10%.

3. **Post-traumatic stress disorder**

Post-traumatic stress disorder (PTSD) is a mental health condition that comes from experiencing a distressing, shocking, or traumatic event. PTSD is considered a "high value" disability because veterans can get up to 100% permanent and total, along with many other benefits. In order to get service-connected for PTSD, veterans must have:

A. A current diagnosis of PTSD from a mental health doctor that shows veteran is still getting current treatment.

B. An in-service event "stressor letter" written by the veteran for combat incidents. Or veterans can have a stressor letter for non-combat events.

C. A nexus opinion letter from doctor linking the current diagnosis of PTSD and the in-service event.

Veterans are encouraged to file a claim for PTSD immediately after returning from deployment because the VA looks at the one-year period after returning home from deployment as the most crucial period in determining what rating to award the veteran! In my case, I applied for PTSD after returning back home from Iraq but was denied at the regional office. So I appealed and the judge awarded me 30% automatically, based on the law at that time which states any veteran deployed to combat with DD-214 showing proof of combat would receive 30% for PTSD.

4. **Scars, general**

Veterans are eligible to receive service connection for scars that resulted from their time in military service or from a service-connected condition that required surgery. Scars can be secondary to surgeries. In other words, the surgery caused the veteran to get another condition. The ratings for scars are very low. This is a low-value disability that carries little weight when trying to obtain 100%, but helps when adding all your conditions together. You must have more than one or two scars that are painful or unstable. The VA rates scars based on the percentage of the body that is covered.

5. **Limitation of flexion, knee**

   Limitation of flexion of the knee is one type of knee condition that can receive service connection. This condition occurs when the range of motion of the knee is limited. The VA does not consider the pain level but instead the veteran is awarded based on range of motion, which is usually 10%.

6. **Lumbosacral or cervical strain**

   This refers to back and neck pain. These conditions are usually rated based on limitation of motion pertaining to forward flexion or how far the veteran can bend over. I was awarded 20% the first time, then my condition got worse. Three years later, I was awarded 40% based on the rating scale for a back condition. The most the VA will award a veteran is 40% for a back condition, unless the veteran is basically paralyzed. I consider back claims a high-value claim to pursue if the back pain stems from physical training, heavy gear, and lack of proper shoes while in service.

7. **Paralysis of the sciatic nerve**

   Paralysis of the sciatic nerve is very common among veterans, mainly due to the fact that the nerves are linked to back and neck issues. When the VA rates a veteran's back and neck conditions, they must rate any neurological residuals. Therefore, paralysis of the sciatic nerve is often granted without the veteran having to file additional claims. This happened to me when I appealed all my claims to a judge in Washington DC. I did not apply for paralysis of the sciatic nerve, but the judge awarded me 10% in both lower legs as secondary to back pain. This pain starts in the lower back and shoots all the way down the back of the thighs to the calves, then to the bottom of both feet. In most cases, a veteran will get 10% for sciatic nerve pain.

8. **Limitation of range of motion of the ankle**

   The VA mainly looks for diagnostic code 5271 when rating limitation of motion of the ankle. Your doctor must assign this code in the nexus letter. The rating criteria deals with the range of motion of the ankle. Veterans are usually rated at 10%, which consists of "moderate symptomology" while a 20% rating consists of "marked conditions."

9. **Migraines**

   Migraines are recurring, intense, and happen on a frequent basis, which can be debilitating. Sometimes migraines cause people to lock themselves in a room of complete darkness with no sound. Even more, it prevents people from living their normal day-to-day life. Migraines are considered a high-value claim! For service connection for migraines, veterans are usually rated under diagnostic code 8100 based on the frequency, severity, duration, and impact on daily life. All of these requirements are located in the Federal Veterans Laws, Rules and Regulations book.

   In addition to direct service connection, veterans may also receive service connection for their migraines on a secondary basis. If you have a separate service-connected condition that then causes or aggravates your migraine condition, then a secondary service connection may be warranted. For example, a neck strain can be so painful that over time it leads to intense migraine headaches. In this case, link or cause and effect of migraine headaches to service-connected orthopedic condition must be proven in order to receive VA disability benefits.

10. **Degenerative arthritis of the spine**

    Degenerative arthritis of the spine rating criteria is determined based on the joint and whether it is a major or minor. Veterans are normally not rated under arthritis diagnostic code because it would cause a lower rating. But if the veteran also has a limited range of motion or incapacitating episodes, it could result in a higher rating based on the VA manual. The doctor must have this written down in a nexus letter concerning the veteran's condition.

11. **Hypertension or high blood pressure**

High blood pressure can lead to heart attacks, kidney failure, and heart strokes. Symptoms of hypertension (high blood pressure) include chest pain, severe headaches, vision problems, fatigue, difficulty breathing, blood in urine, irregular heartbeat, and pounding in the chest and neck area.

Body systems that are rated for disability

Veterans can apply and get disabilities in 15 different categories in order to become service-connected. I recommend you research and study each category to get a better understanding of your conditions. It will help when discussing your condition with the doctor. For every disability, there is a rating chart on the VA website with rules and regulations: **https://www.benefits.va.gov/warms/bookc.asp**

In a sense, you have to be able to speak the vocabulary to the nurses and doctors because they document what you describe to them. The words you use can be used in your favor or against you when the regional office is making a decision to award or deny benefits.

In each category, there are several diagnoses and descriptions of different conditions. Learn the descriptions and vocabulary so that when you talk to the doctor, you can get the correct diagnosis for your condition, which is a must for each disability. Learning the diagnoses can give you knowledge of the regulations for each disability you are applying for. Also, you'll know if VA rated you properly based on the rating scale for each disability. The 15 body systems are as follows:

1. Respiratory
2. Systemic
3. Auditory
4. Visual
5. Musculoskeletal
6. Hemic
7. Gynecological
8. Genitourinary
9. Digestive
10. Cardiovascular
11. Dental/oral
12. Mental disorders
13. Neurological
14. Endocrine
15. Skin and scars

VA rating chart and symptoms

The VA has a rating scale matched with symptoms for every disability you can apply for. It is to the veteran's advantage to learn the symptoms of each condition you're seeking compensation for. Each rating chart lists in detail what symptoms are expected in order to get a rating increase. To research typical symptoms, simply log onto the internet and search, for example, "symptoms of PTSD." For each rating, the VA will assign the veteran a disability based on what he/she tells the doctor they're experiencing. The veteran's doctor will review the rating chart and use it as a guide to write a nexus letter for the veteran. Again, it's to your advantage to learn the VA rating scale and educate yourself before applying for a disability. Also, you must learn the codes and inform your doctor of which benefit or what percentage you are seeking.

For the VA regional office to determine what percentage to assign the veteran, they must receive a nexus letter stating the veteran's disability is likely due to military service. The letter must include at least a paragraph that matches the rating scale for the particular disability the veteran is seeking. The regional office always considers whether or not the doctor's comments reflect the symptoms written on the VA rating chart.

By understanding the VA rating chart, I was able to educate my private doctors who did not have experience in writing VA nexus letters and matching it up to the VA rating charts, which helps veterans get disability or a rating increase.

Veterans are assigned a 0, 30, 50, or 100% rating depending on the severity of their condition. Veterans should learn the symptoms for each percentage that the regional office looks for when determining what percentage to award the veteran. For example, if you have sleep apnea, you can simply log online and type "VA rating scale for sleep apnea" and it will give you the diagnosis and codes. Also, the rating scale for sleep apnea gives step-by-step instructions when seeking a higher rating.

Low-value claims vs High-value claims

Low-value claims are considered to be 20% or less. On the other hand, a high-value claim is considered 30% or higher. **The quickest way to obtain 100% rating mathematically is to first seek high-value claims!** And if you are already service connected for a condition, you can also seek secondary conditions to boost your overall rating to approximately 180% or 200% to equal 100% P&T.

The largest category of service-connected disabilities come from musculoskeletal problems, which consists of 40% of all disabilities that veterans apply for. So a good starting point would be to apply for disabilities that are in the musculoskeletal system. This includes impairment of knees and arthritis due to trauma, back pain, shoulder pain, neck pain, etc. Veterans should plan and strategize by studying **the US code of federal regulations: www.ecfr.gov** for each disability. **All disabilities are not rated the same!** You should learn which disabilities have the highest rating to apply for first and learn the eligibility requirements, symptoms, and the rating chart for each disability. Every step up the chart results in an increase until veteran reaches 100% permanent & total. Any conditions you were treated for while on active duty are a starting point if you do not know what disability to apply for. Get copies of your medical records and look for all the diagnoses the doctors have documented in your record.

Veterans who are seeking 100% P&T from the VA must have at least a total overall rating of 160% after adding all your ratings together. If you decide to go this route, I suggest seeking 200% schedular rating because the VA math will reduce your overall rating down to almost 100%. You must learn the difference between low-value claims and high-value claims. By studying the maximum rating for each disability, you position yourself with a head start in the game to earn increased ratings over the years until the VA awards you permanent and total status.

16

Once a veteran has had a rating for twenty years, by law the VA must award him/her permanent and total. So, the veteran has twenty years to get the maximum rating possible. Veterans can also strategize by learning which disabilities have high-value claims, which would reduce the number of years in getting 100% P&T. Many veterans spend years fighting the VA to get a rating increase on their claims with the hope of getting 100 P&T. But they don't understand that their disabilities were maxed out years ago at 10%, 20%, or 30%. The VA does not explain this to veterans.

There are some low-value claims that the highest rating you can get is between 10%-30%. However, you can apply for a secondary condition. For example, tinnitus is considered a low-value claim. But you can claim that the tinnitus caused a secondary condition: "service connection for migraine headaches, secondary to service-connected tinnitus."

A veteran must have been rated for a low-value claim before applying for secondary claims that can put them over the hump and eventually 100% especially if he/she is 80% or 90%. The VA math is complicated. Technically, a veteran will need a 50% rating to move up from 90% to 100%. Many veterans are not educated on the VA math and low-value claims vs high-value claims. Once they learn the highest rating for each disability they're claiming, they will be able to figure out strategies of which claims to apply for that are "high-value claims" to get them to 100%. Then they can apply for secondary conditions once they have 80% or 90%. It's very difficult to get 100% once you reach 90%. A backdoor option to getting paid at 100% level is to apply for TDIU if you have one disability at 60% or higher.

Now, some **high-value claims** to consider when first applying include:

- Migraine headaches - maximum rating 50%
- Hypertension or high blood pressure - maximum rating 60%
- Sleep apnea as a secondary to PTSD - maximum rating 50%, with a c-pap machine 100%
- Fibromyalgia - maximum rating 40%

- Diabetes mellitus - maximum rating 100%
- Adjustment disorder with anxiety - 100%
- Rheumatoid arthritis - maximum rating 100%
- Hernia hiatal - maximum rating 60%
- Foot drop - maximum rating 40%
- Paralysis of sciatic nerve - maximum rating 80%
- Back pain - maximum rating 100%
- Intervertebral disc syndrome (VDS) - maximum rating 60%
- Gerd acid reflux - maximum rating 80%
- Irritable bowel syndrome - maximum rating 30%
- Somatic fatigue syndrome - maximum rating 80% to 100%

Secondary claims - you must already be rated for a service-connected disability before applying for secondary conditions:

- Depression or anxiety, secondary to physical injuries
- Traumatic brain injury (TBI) - maximum rating up to 100%
- Total disability individual unemployability or IU - veteran must have one disability rated at 60% or higher such as PTSD or any mental condition or physical condition that prevents veteran from obtaining or keeping a job due to military service. More detail on TDIU in a later chapter.
- Post-traumatic stress disorder (PTSD) - maximum rating of 100% P&T ($3,000/month from VA and social security benefits for combat veterans)
- Anxiety and depression - maximum rating of 100% P&T ($3,000/ month from VA and social security benefits for non-combat veterans)

Personality disorder

The VA does not recognize personality disorder as a disability. So do not file a claim for personality disorder. Typically, if veterans get treatment from psychologists before entering the military, the VA will write a denial letter due to personality disorder. The VA tries to focus on the veteran's childhood to prevent awarding the veteran with a mental health claim. So, veterans must know *not* to apply for personality disorder. It will be a waste of your time!

Federal Veterans' Laws, Rules and Regulations

I recommend all veterans purchase "Federal Veterans' Laws, Rules, and Regulations 2019-2020 edition" from Amazon for $84. This book of laws is written by Congress to govern all veterans' benefits administrations and hospitals to ensure equal access and representation of all veterans without discrimination based on race or disability. You can also study the laws and regulations on the VA's website: **benefit.va.gov.** If you don't know your rights, you have no rights. Before seeking benefits, read your bible. It can save you a lot of time and a lot of hassle dealing with the VA regional office.

From my experience working at the Veterans Benefits Administration and as a veteran seeking benefits myself, I witnessed veterans being denied benefits simply because the veterans do not know the laws, rules, and regulations set by Congress. That's why I suggest purchasing this book off Amazon. It was a game changer for me. And it helped me to appeal my claims four times to the judge in Washington DC. I won every case without a lawyer because I read the VA manual and did my homework. As a result of 21 years fighting the VA for my hard-earned benefits, I finally reached my highest rating of 90% total disability individual unemployability (TDIU) with permanent and total (P&T) status.

"The Federal Veterans Laws, Rules and Regulations" is a resource book that offers quick reference to important federal statutes and regulations contained in title 38 of the United States Code Service (USCS) and the Code of Federal Regulations (CFR), as well as all of the rules of the United States Court of Appeals for Veterans Claims. The statutes and regulations included in this book cover almost all issues concerning:

- Service-connected compensation benefits
- Service-connected death benefits (dependency and indemnity compensation benefits)

- Non-service-connected pension benefits
- Non-service-connected death pension benefits
- VA medical care (hospital, nursing home, domiciliary and medical care)
- Insurance benefits
- Specially adapted housing benefits
- Burial benefits
- Burial in a national cemetery
- Education assistance
- Educational assistance for survivors and dependents
- Vocational rehabilitation
- Automobiles and adaptive equipment
- Job counseling and job placement
- Employment and training
- Veterans reemployment rights
- Effective dates of benefit payment for correct "back payment"
- Appellate rights and due process
- The rules governing the adjudication of claims for VA benefits
- Rules governing the VA accreditation of agents and attorneys
- The complete schedule for rating disabilities (38 CFR part iv)

eBenefits: https://www.eBenefits.va.gov

eBenefits provides resources and self-service capabilities to military personnel, veterans, and their families to access, apply, research, and manage their VA and military benefits. There has been a big effort to put a variety of resources all together in one location to reduce the stress on veterans seeking benefits from different agencies! Service members and veterans must register for an eBenefits account at one of two levels: basic or premium. A premium account gives you full access to personal data in VA and DOD systems, including applying for benefits online. You can contact veterans' affairs eBenefits support at 800-983-0937.

With eBenefits, veterans can:

1. Submit claims for benefits and/or upload documents directly to the VA
2. Track status of claim and appeals
3. Print VA letters
4. VA prescription refills
5. VA appointments
6. Pension benefits
7. Secure messaging on myhealthevet to nurse and doctor
8. DOD Tricare health insurance
9. Add or change dependents
10. Education benefits for veterans and dependents - chapter 35
11. Transfer entitlement of post-9/11 GI bill to eligible dependents (service members only)
12. Access military personnel documents such as form DD-214, certificate of release or discharge from active duty
13. Obtain a VA-guaranteed home loan certificate of eligibility which allows veteran to purchase homes with no down payment

14. Update your contact and direct deposit information for certain benefits.
15. Register for VA healthcare treatment at local VA medical center – VA form 10-10EZ or call 877-222-8387
16. Request a veteran's service officer to represent you
17. Obtain verification of military service, civil service preference, or VA benefits.

Forms and documents required in veteran's claim: VSO representatives

When veterans first apply for VA benefits, they choose a power of attorney by filling out VA form 21-22, appointment of individual as claimant's representative. They are employed at the Veterans Benefits Administration to assist veterans in developing their claims. Some states do not have veterans' organizations. The power of attorneys employed at the VBA do not charge veterans to help in getting benefits because they are employed by the VA. Veterans have the option to select a Veterans Service Organization (VSO) to help them throughout the process or the veteran can choose to do it by themselves. Some VSO are not as proficient as others when it comes to knowing all the laws concerning veterans' benefits set by Congress.

The VSO makes decisions on behalf of the veteran, similar to a lawyer. They may also accept settlement without asking the veteran and will notify the veteran at a later date. This can work in favor of veterans or against the veterans. This is why veterans must read and study the VA laws, rules and regulations for themselves. From my experience in dealing with the VA, many VSO's knowledge are limited to what the supervisors want them to know. You should never put total trust in anyone when it comes to obtaining VA benefits.

Here are a few veterans service organizations you can choose from:

- Disabled American Veterans (DAV)
- Veterans of Foreign Wars (VFW)
- Paralyzed Veterans of America (PVA)
- American Vets
- American Gulf War Veterans association
- Blinded Veterans Association

- Military Order of the Purple Heart
- National Association for Uniformed SVCS
- The Retired Enlisted Association
- Veterans and Families
- Vietnam Veterans of America
- World War II US Veterans Association

VA form 21-686c - declaration of status of dependent

It is very important to turn in VA form 21-686c when first applying for disability because if you are awarded a disability, the VA will have to back pay you, including dependents, beginning at 30% rate or higher. You must submit to the VA the following documents: marriage certificate, children's birth certificate, and veteran's birth certificate.

The fastest way to add a dependent is online through eBenefits.com if you have set up a premium account. A decision can be made within 48 hours. The VA form 21-686c must be filled out and signed. Veterans who are rated at 30% or higher are eligible to file a claim for additional disability compensation to get a higher payment for a child or spouse. Also, you can file a claim to add parents as a dependent by completing VA form 21-509. A dependent is considered:

1. A spouse (including spouses of same-sex marriages and common-law marriages)
2. Children (including biological children, stepchildren, and adopted children) who are unmarried and either:
   A. Under the age of 18
   B. Between the ages of 18-23 and attending school full-time, or
   C. Who were seriously disabled before the age of 18
3. Parents who are in your direct care and whose income and net worth are below the limit set by law

DD 214 – certificate of release or discharge from active duty

The DD-214 is one of the most important documents when applying for disability. There are codes on the veteran's DD-214 that indicate whether the veteran is a combat veteran, what medals the veteran received (which should make the process of qualifying for disability easier), 10-point preference when applying for federal jobs, and what military/civilian related jobs the veteran qualifies for. You can also use DD-214 to apply for GI bill benefits while in college.

Veterans can request copies of their DD-214 or DD-215 report of separation by getting an eBenefits premium account. Go to www.eBenefits.va.gov and register. After you have registered for a premium account, click on the "manage benefits" tab and go to the military personnel file (DPRIS) link to request a copy of the DD-214. If your records were damaged or destroyed in the 1973 fire, the National Personnel Records Center (NPRC) might be able to use alternate sources to reconstruct service data and document military service. If you served before records were scanned into the computer system, log on to www.archives.gov/veterans and click on the "request military records online" tab. You will be able to:

1. Request service records online, by mail, or by fax
2. Request medical and health records
3. Check the status of an existing request
4. More ways to get service records
5. Recently separated veteran
6. Replace lost medals and awards
7. Funeral home director information page

VA form 21-526EZ - application for disability compensation

VA form 21-526EZ – application for disability compensation and related compensation benefits – is used to file for different types of disabilities. The list of disability options veterans can apply for include the following:

- Disability service connection
- Increased disability compensation
- Secondary service compensation
- Individual unemployability
- Special monthly compensation
- Automobile allowance
- Temporary total disability
- Benefits based on a veteran's seriously disabled child
- Specially adapted housing/special home adaptation
- Adaptive equipment compensation under 38 u.s.c. 1151

The VA form 526EZ must be filled out and signed. This starts the application process for compensation. You may list several disabilities you're seeking on the same 526EZ form. It can be filled out online through eBenefits or mailed in to your local VBA regional office or to the VA Evidence Intake Center. If you hand deliver it to the VBA regional office, they will date stamp it, which will determine your starting pay date if you are awarded benefits. Sometimes the VA loses paperwork, but you will have proof you turned the form in if you have to dispute it later on.

As a former employee at the regional office, I have seen veterans' applications for benefits lost while other veterans' paperwork was shredded, like mine was. It makes the numbers look good and therefore the staff at the VA get bonuses at the end of the year for great work! With that said, I recommend to always follow up to check the status of your claim or appeal on a weekly basis. This is a very important part of the process. By doing so, you're holding the VA accountable and you are taking ownership of your claim!

When I first applied 21 years ago, it took an average of 1.5 years to receive a decision, but now the VA goal is 90 days. There was a time a veteran could just write a letter stating he wants to file a claim, but as of recent, the VA now requires you to fill out a form for every claim to avoid confusion when the veteran service representative (VSR) processes your applications.

When filling out the 21-526 EZ, make sure the following information is correct:

A. What disabilities you are claiming
B. How you are claiming these disabilities
   1. Direct service connection - injuries happened in the military
   2. Increase - you're already service-connected but your disability has gotten worse so you're requesting a rating increase
   3. Aggravated - military progressed an existing disability beyond its normal progression
   4. Secondary disability - you have developed a new injury as a result of a service-connected disability
   5. Disability due to exposure - Agent Orange, Gulf War, mustard gas, asbestos, etc.

Write the correct word of conditions you're claiming for disability

Many veterans don't know how to word the correct conditions they are claiming on their application for compensation. This is the 'VA language' raters look for on veterans' applications for compensation. I will list a few claims and secondary conditions I'm aware of that veterans can use to file their primary claim and secondary conditions on VA **form 526EZ- application for disability compensation and related compensation benefits.** Both are necessary and can help you get permanent and total quicker!

It is best to use private doctors who will work in your best interest, especially when it comes time to appeal the VA's decisions. The VA regional office and the VA doctors work for the same agency. And some VA doctors will not write nexus letters! You should write the exact words on your application for compensation form to help the rater understand what disabilities you are seeking:

Some examples of primary claims to file:

- "service connection for cancer" - primary care doctor
- "service connection for Agent Orange" - primary care doctor
- "service connection for headaches" - neurologist
- "service connection for diabetes" - primary care doctor
- "service connection for asthma and chronic bronchitis"
- "service connection for neck pain" - primary care doctor or chiropractor
- "service connection for shoulder pain" – primary care doctor or chiropractor
- "service connection for back pain" – primary care doctor or chiropractor
- "service connection for hypertension or high blood pressure" - primary care doctor or heart specialist

- "service connection for chronic back" - primary care or chiropractor
- "service connection for obstructive sleep apnea" - pulmonary and sleep specialist
- "service connection for flat feet" – podiatrist
- "service connection for military sexual trauma (MST)" - psychologist
- "service connection for somatic symptom disorder" - psychologist
- "service connection for lifestyle impact claim (non-combat)" - psychologist
- "service connection for anxiety" – psychologist
- "service connection for depression" – psychologist
- "service connection for post-traumatic stress disorder (PTSD)" - psychologist

Some examples of secondary claims to file:

- "service connection for depression, as secondary to back pain" – mental health doctor
- "service connection for headaches, as secondary to service-connected PTSD" – mental health doctor
- "service connection for major depressive disorder, as secondary to service-connected PTSD" – mental health doctor
- "service connection for anxiety, as secondary to service-connected PTSD" – mental health doctor
- "service connection for major depressive disorder, as secondary to service-connected PTSD" – mental health doctor
- "service connection for obstructive sleep apnea, as secondary to post-traumatic stress disorder based on this author's IMO" – mental health doctor
- "service connection for obstructive sleep apnea, as secondary to service-connected headaches/migraines" – mental health doctor
- "service connection for headaches, as secondary to service-connected tinnitus" – mental health doctor

- "service connection for disability in neck pain, as secondary to chronic back" - chiropractor
- "service connection for cervical spine disability, as secondary to service-connected chronic back" - chiropractor
- "service connection for obstructive sleep apnea, as secondary to service-connected cervical spine abnormalities" - chiropractor
- "service connection for knee joint arthritis, as secondary to plantar fasciitis (flat feet)" - chiropractor
- "service connection for foot drop, as secondary to service-connected chronic back" - chiropractor

Bilateral conditions = 2 disabilities

- "service connection for sciatica nerve disability in left leg, as secondary to service-connected chronic back"
- "service connection for sciatica nerve disability in right leg, as secondary to service-connected chronic back"
- "service connection for plantar fasciitis and/or foot problems in left foot, due to chronic pain"
- "service connection for plantar fasciitis and/or foot problems in right foot, due to chronic pain"
- "service connection for depression and anxiety resulting from service-connected ringing in both ears" (secondary mental health claim)
- "service connection for erectile dysfunction, as secondary to service connected back pain from pain medication" – primary care doctor
- "service connection for sleep apnea, secondary to hypertension" - sleep specialist
- "service connection for hypertension, secondary to sleep apnea" - sleep specialist
- "service connection for erectile dysfunction, as secondary to service-connected chronic back pain" – primary care doctor
- "service connection for erectile dysfunction, as secondary to service-connected sleep apnea" – primary care doctor

- "service connection for erectile dysfunction, as secondary to service-connected hypertension" – primary care doctor
- "service connection for erectile dysfunction, as secondary to service-connected PTSD" – primary care doctor
- "service connection for headaches, as secondary to service-connected neck injury" – primary care doctor
- "service connection for insomnia, as secondary to tinnitus" - sleep specialist
- "service connection for obstructive sleep apnea, as secondary to asthma based on this author's IMO" – primary care doctor
- "service connection for obstructive sleep apnea, as secondary to service-connected sinusitis, rhinitis, deviated septum" – primary care doctor
- "service connection for obstructive sleep apnea, as secondary to service-connected cardiovascular disease" – primary care doctor
- "service connection for obstructive sleep apnea, as secondary to service-connected lung disease" – primary care doctor
- "service connection for obstructive sleep apnea, as secondary to service-connected antidepressants" – primary care doctor
- "service connection for obstructive sleep apnea, as secondary to service-connected upper airway resistance syndrome" – primary care doctor
- "service connection for obstructive sleep apnea, as secondary to service-connected fibromyalgia" – primary care doctor
- "service connection for obstructive sleep apnea, as secondary to service-connected stroke and ischemic heart disease (GERD)" – primary care doctor
- "service connection for obstructive sleep apnea, as secondary to service-connected chronic obstructive pulmonary disease (COPD)/asthma" – primary care doctor
- "service connection for obstructive sleep apnea, as secondary to service-connected cardiovascular disease" – primary care doctor
- "service connection for obstructive sleep apnea, as secondary to service-connected diabetes mellitus" – primary care doctor

Tip: please note that it is very difficult to get sleep apnea as a primary claim. Reports show that 3 out of 4 veterans are denied for sleep apnea as a primary claim because they do not have a c-pap machine. However, there is a way around this: you can apply for sleep apnea as a secondary claim in which a service-connected disability that you are already getting compensated for caused sleep apnea to develop. To make it easier, I have listed above several service-connected conditions that can cause sleep apnea to develop. You must already be service-connected for the conditions above before filing sleep apnea as a secondary claim. This is another game changer - a veteran can get 50% sleep apnea secondary to a service-connected disability!!! Any primary claim or secondary condition that is rated 30% or above is considered a "high-value" claim to pursue to get to 100% P&T.

VA medical records -
https://myhealth.va.gov

Veterans can use myhealth.va.gov to send private, secure email messages to their nurse or doctor without visiting the hospital. **By sending secure messages regarding pain level and symptoms via e-mail, your message becomes part of your VA medical records.** And when the regional office reviews your medical records to determine eligibility for disability, they will look to see if veteran ever complains to their doctor and how often to determine if it's a chronic condition. Some veterans do not complain at all because the military has taught us to be a man and tough it out, **go to the doctor at least two times a year stating your pain level.**

In addition to sending secure emails to document your pain level, you can also **call the local VA medical center to speak to someone in the call center who will type your pain level and all your symptoms over the phone and send an e-mail to your doctor or nurse. And when your nurse or doctor responds back, those notes and inquiry become medical evidence in your medical records.** This is one way to get a diagnosis for the disability you are seeking. This is another game changer! You can request medical records, make appointments, send secure messages, and review your VA health records at myhealth.va.gov.

How to request medical records

You can request medical records in person at the regional office or a limited copy at the VA hospital. The hospital will give you only medical records from the past year or two. To get your military records, which are located based on which branch of service you were in and based on what time frame you were active duty, simply fill out **SF 180 - request military personnel records.** Include all your active duty periods of service and reserve periods on the original application. **Include DD-214 (discharge papers),** then mail the signed VA form SF-180 to the military branch you selected. It usually takes a few months to receive your military records.

The VA has an obligation to write to you informing you of what they have received on your behalf. If your military records were destroyed in a fire, VA must tell you. On July 12, 1973, the National Personnel Records Center (NPRC) experienced a fire that destroyed approximately 16-18 million military personnel files. Unfortunately, there were no duplicate copies or microfilm created for those records. That's why it's very important to keep original copies in a safe location because many years later you will need copies to file disabilities and appeal your denied letters from the regional office. It took me several months to receive my military records from St. Louis National Archive Records. Then I gave copies to the regional office. Never give your original copies, always keep the original!

Tip: The VA regional office takes into consideration if you are taking medication and using prosthetic devices such as a walking cane or dolomite walker-wheelchair, back brace, knee braces, c-pap machine for sleep apnea, blood pressure monitoring device for hypertension or high blood pressure, etc. All of these devices can help you in getting the highest compensation rating possible, if your doctor has prescribed them and they are documented in your c-file as evidence!

You can obtain a copy of your claims folder by submitting a written FOIA (freedom of information act) request to the VA by mail or fax.

Complete SF-180 - request pertaining to VA records and send to both addresses below with the following statement:

"I am requesting a copy of my entire claims folder, including all military personal records, service treatment records, rating decisions, rating code sheets, compensation, and pension exams from the VA and/or third party contractors such as QTC and any other information in my electronic claims folder not listed above."

Department of Veterans Affairs
Claims Intake Center
P.O. box 5235
Janesville, Wisconsin 53547-5235

Fax #: 1-844-531-7818

Also, you can ask for this information to be on paper or on a disc. The regional office will request copies, but it's quicker to request copies and then submit them to the regional office.

How to request military service records

Veterans can request their military records by contacting the National Personnel Records Center. Requests should be mailed to the following address:

National Personnel Records Center
1 Archives Drive
St. Louis, MO 63138

Or, to request records telephonically or via e-mail:

phone: 314-801-0800
email: mpr.center@nara.gov
website: archives.gov

How to correct military service records

Veterans can request corrections to their military service records by completing DD form 149-Application for correction of military record under the provisions of title 10, U.S. code, section 1552. You may complete the form and mail it to the appropriate address of the branch the veteran served in which is located at the bottom of the second page.

Tricare online

Service members on active duty or reserve can utilize Tricare online. **Please go to sick call while on active duty, see private doctors, and have your reserve unit activated to have medical conditions documented in your VA's c-file and military medical records because you will need these medical records later in life when you apply for disability with the VA and/or Department of Defense before exiting the military.**

I recall going to doctors while on active duty serving in the U.S. Army and when my Air National Guard unit was deployed to Iraq in 2003. I made sure I went to sick call to complain about my sleep apnea problems, back pain, foot pain, and PTSD. I had all my conditions documented while I was on active duty and I continued to get ongoing treatment at the VA hospital and private doctors even after I was discharged from active duty and discharged from the guard. I knew the laws before I applied for disabilities and it helped me to understand the process and the rules of the game when it came to fighting the VA regional office for my benefits. By going to the doctor before and after discharge from the military, it shows a continuation of medical treatments.

If there are no medical records showing the soldier went on sick call or visited any doctor while on active duty, the VA usually denies the veteran for lack of medical evidence. If a veteran was activated and deployed to a combat zone, it is highly unlikely the veteran was able to see a doctor. So Congress wrote into law that it should be easier for veterans to get benefits, meaning there should be fewer requirements to prove their conditions are service-related if the veteran seeks treatment immediately after returning from deployment. **It is very important to see private doctors or VA doctors immediately after returning home from deployment (within the first year) and continue to get ongoing treatment until you die to prove you have a disability(s).** This was another game changer in obtaining my disability benefits.

Visit the Tricare website at: tricareonline.com. You can instantly access military treatment facility healthcare records for up to the last 30 years. There are three ways to log on: DS login, CAC card, or my-pay password. You will be able to make appointments, refill prescriptions, contact the nurse advice line, send a secure message to your doctor, request service separation information, and blue button to select all from the past 30 years to download medical records in pdf version onto the eBenefits website.

Physical therapy

Veterans can get physical therapy for about three to four months by requesting their primary care doctor put in a consult or referral at the VA hospital. Veterans are encouraged to get treatment from their private doctors to get a second opinion, especially when appealing their claims to the Board of Veterans' Affairs.

Physical therapy treats veterans with various musculoskeletal dysfunctions. If you are seeking disability for back pain, the physical therapist will check to feel if there is tightness or muscle spasms. This was a game changer in getting my disability for back pain! The VA regional office checks whether or not you are getting extra treatment for your conditions that you are applying for.

Prosthetic and sensory aids

Veterans can get medically prescribed prosthetic and sensory aids by requesting their primary doctors to put a consult or referral at the VA hospital. He/she can then pick up the devices that will assist them in daily activities. These aids include: hearing aids, eyeglasses, orthopedic braces and shoes, crutches and canes, artificial limbs, communication aids, and wheelchairs.

In order to be eligible for VA benefits and services, your discharge status must be a condition other than dishonorable, unless the VA regional office makes an exception. You must have a service-connected disability, injury or illness which results in the need for prosthetic aid. The VA regional office takes that into consideration what disability rating to award you, especially when you are seeking an increase in your disability rating. This can be a game changer for veterans!

Emergency room

Veterans can get treatment for urgent needs and emergency conditions for many illnesses and injuries including those that are life threatening. If the condition is not life threatening, the emergency room may refer you back to your primary doctor. The emergency room is open 24 hours a day, 7 days a week. Veterans are eligible to visit the emergency room three times a year without co-pays, at no cost to Medicare if the veteran is 50% or higher, individual unemployable (IU-TDIU), or permanent and total.

On the other hand, if veteran is permanent and total or TDIU, the VA will provide home nursing care and they can get emergency care for any disability outside the VA hospital at the VA's expense if the VA was not able to provide care in a timely manner. I remember going to the emergency room several times for several conditions that I later applied for disabilities. I recall going to the emergency room on holidays while people were out celebrating. I was very sick from serving in the military. If you do not live near a VA medical center, you are encouraged to visit your private doctor or a hospital near your residence.

One tip of advice: always get more than one doctor's opinion. Because I had health insurance, I sought treatment from private doctors to counter the VA doctors. From my experience, the VA medical center will treat a veteran, but when it comes down to getting a nexus letter or appealing your case, the VA doctors will not be there to help the veteran win their disabilities because of liability issues. As a result of not getting nexus letters from VA doctors, I had to seek treatment from private doctors for the same conditions I was treated for at the VA hospital.

This was a game changer because the regional office reviews the veteran's file to see whether or not he/she went to the emergency room and how often for a potential service-connected condition. There's a law in the VA rules and regulations that states if two doctors have different opinions about the veteran's condition, the adjudicator at the regional office must give the benefit of the doubt in the veteran's favor. Be advised this usually doesn't happen because many veterans do not know and understand all the laws that govern the VA regional office and veterans' rights. I had to file four appeals in 21 years. Every time the VA regional office called me in for C&P exams, they always denied me with false excuses. But I appealed to the judge in Washington, DC because the regional office never gave me fair due process or the benefit of the doubt. I never lost a case in court!

Nexus letter from doctor

A nexus letter is a document that a doctor or other medical professional writes for a veteran that explains that the veteran's condition is related to their military service. This nexus letter can make the difference between an award or denial for disability benefits. Keep in mind that VA doctors are hesitant to write a nexus letter or independent medical opinion.

Many times, veterans are denied compensation because of lack of qualifications of the Veteran Service Officers (VSO) who assist the veteran in putting their claims together at the regional office. Most VSO do not have medical backgrounds, and there's no doctor or medical professional to assist and interpret the doctor's medical reports. Likewise, VA raters who make decisions on whether to grant disability or deny a veteran must still review and assess medical evidence provided by doctors and a QTC examiner to determine what percentage of disability to give the veteran. In most cases, the VA denies veterans without understanding the doctor's diagnosis.

A nexus letter from a doctor should address, but is not limited to: diagnosis, complaints, pain level, examination plan of care, prognosis, functional loss, functional impairment, occupational and social impairments, x-ray and MRI with range of motion measurement from chiropractor, medical devices for high blood pressure, and devices to assist in walking such as cane, wheelchair, back brace, knee brace, and massager pad. A nexus letter is one of the most important documents that helps veteran qualify for VA disability, but the regional office will not tell the veteran this. And the VA doctors will not provide nexus letters for veterans in most cases because it is a conflict of interest to help the veteran while at the same time hurting the VA's budget when veteran is approved for benefits.

As a result of VA doctors not providing nexus letters, I recommend getting private doctors for each disability to work on your behalf to provide a nexus letter. After getting private doctors to provide nexus letters, the VA will then get opinions from their doctors in effort to counter the veteran's private doctors to prevent veteran from being approved for disability.

As I mentioned before, when there are different medical opinions from more than one doctor, the law states the tie breaker goes to the veteran. However, in most cases, the regional office does not play by the rules. This happened to me. When the regional office denied me, despite all the medical evidence, I filed an appeal to the board in Washington, DC and won my case. I had all the proper medical evidence and the regional office still rejected what I submitted and kept denying me for every C&P exam. So I used my insurance to get treatment from private doctors who worked in my interest.

As a former Veterans' Benefits Administration employee, I have witnessed how the VA screws veterans over because veterans do not know the laws written by Congress to protect veterans' rights. I was there in the situation room. I would attend weekly staff meetings with supervisors and the rating specialists to determine how many veterans were approved and how many veterans were denied in the past month. The managers would get big bonuses at the end of the year for all the veterans that were denied. I was a clerk at the time, not knowing what was going on. My supervisor gave the clerks around $200. I thought it was for my good work ethics. Nope. I have seen directors steal millions of dollars of taxpayers' money that were for veterans' disabilities. This is a shame and a disgrace to all veterans who have served and sacrificed for our country!

All of my success in getting a permanent & total status came from private doctors who worked in my best interest. In order for a doctor to write nexus letters for each disability a veteran is claiming, the veteran must submit all of his/her medical records to their doctor: diagnosis or list of problems, nursing notes, operation report, discharge report, hospital admission medical exam and history report, lab test results, x-ray, cat scan summaries, MRI, all medications prescribed, social security award letter, employer disability award letter, etc. Veterans can submit a nexus letter anytime during the application process. But the sooner, the better!

If the VA denies you, the VA will not tell you it's because there was no nexus letter, but will make up something in placement of the nexus letter. The VA regional office will send a denial letter that says: "You have been denied because we could not determine a connection to military service." Instead of saying "There's no nexus letter." The VA constantly gives veterans the run around and landmines to trip them up to prevent having to pay them!

A nexus letter is a statement describing a veteran's current symptoms. It describes how often he/she experiences symptoms and how long he/she experiences symptom. It is very important that the doctor note in the nexus letter that he or she has reviewed the veteran's entire file and medical records. Failure to do so can result in the VA denying the veteran benefits. In addition, the doctor must be certified in the area of health that is at issue. The doctor must state in the letter whether it is "at least as likely as not" that the current condition was caused by an event during service. Also, using a doctor that has recently performed an examination on the veteran can add weight to the nexus letter in favor of the veteran!

Another element of the nexus letter must include the doctor's references or a medical article relating to the veteran's condition and current diagnosed condition and its relation to the veteran's military service. From my experience, I have had success in dealing with private doctors who are a neutral party in rendering their medical opinion. After studying VA laws, rules, and regulations, I discovered getting my nexus letters for each disability from my private doctors was another game changer for me!

Sample of nexus letter:

*Note: this is not a form to fill out. Please re-type the following information onto your professional letterhead/stationery.

Date _____

Reference (veteran's name) _____

SSN# _____   VA file _____

To whom it may concern,

I am Dr. _____. I am board certified to practice in my specialty. My credentials are included. I have been asked to write a statement in support of the aforementioned veteran's claim.

I have personally reviewed the veteran's VA medical file, service records, and civilian treatment records. He has been compliant with and showed some changes in care. I have also reviewed and have noted the circumstances and events of his military service, which include [name of the event or events you claim are the cause of the condition], in the years _____ [list dates of service] while in military service.

As I re-examined his condition, he/she is having continued difficulty functioning in his/her day-to-day activities, including caring for himself/herself as a direct result of his/her military service-connected disabilities, which are permanent with no possibility of improvement. From a functional standpoint, I do not believe the veteran will be capable of any level of work due to the severity of his/her disabling conditions that are directly related to his/her military service.

Mr./Ms. _____ is a patient under my care since [enter date]. His/her diagnosis is _____ [name the condition].

I am familiar with his/her history and have examined Mr./Ms. _____ often while he/she had been under my care. [specify lab work, x-rays, etc.]

Mr./Ms. _____ has no other known risk factors that may have precipitated his/her current condition.

After a review of the pertinent records, it is my professional opinion that Mr./Ms. _____'s condition is a direct result of his/her [event in service] as due to his/her military service [choose (at least as likely as not) or (more than likely) or (highly likely)]

In my personal experience and in the medical literature, it is known [give a rationale].

Signed,

Dr. _____
[list your credentials and contact information]

50/50 rule

The VA uses a 50/50 rule to determine the validity of claims for service-connected disabilities. When a medical opinion on a veteran is requested by the VA regional office, they will schedule the veteran for a C&P exam. It is in the best interest of the veteran to bring copies of nexus letters to support his/her claims. If the 50/50 rule is not included in the veteran's paperwork for disability, the VA will automatically deny him/her. I recommend veterans bring a copy of their updated nexus letter and the 50/50 statement with current diagnoses to give to the C&P examiner to use in their evaluation report when they submit it to the regional office.

It's always best to be prepared and have copies of updated letters from your treating doctors just in case the VA regional office loses your paperwork. This serves as a backup plan. Another backup plan includes getting your medical records scanned at the VA hospital and faxed or mailed to the VA Evidence Intake Center in Wisconsin. The medical examiner will choose from one of the five following statements when determining if a nexus exists concerning the veteran's diagnosis and military service.

1. "is due to" (100% sure)
2. "more likely than not" (greater than 50%)
3. "at least as likely as not" (equal to or greater than 50%)
4. "not at least as likely as not" (less than 50%)
5. "is not due to" (0%)

If the C&P examiner who works for the VA writes a medical opinion in favor of the veteran, the doctor must give rationale and reasons why a certain disability is one of the following: "is due to, more likely than not, or at least as likely as not."

If the examiner cannot give an opinion, the examiner must state why. If the C&P examiner gives a decision of "not as likely" or "is not due to," then the VA regional office will most likely deny the veteran's claim. The examiner does not determine what rating to give the veteran. The VA regional office makes a decision based on all the evidence. Keep in mind that the opinion of the rating specialist who reviews medical records from veteran's doctors vs the opinion of the C&P examiner may conflict, and the rating specialist, who has the final decision, is not a physician or doctor. This could be grounds to file an appeal if you are denied. I recommend seeking treatment from a private doctor and requesting they **write an independent medical opinion or nexus letter** to counter the VA's C&P examiner, and then hire a VA accredited attorney if you receive a denial letter. A VA lawyer has experience in dealing with a complex and difficult appeals process.

Purpose of an independent medical opinion/nexus letter

The purpose of veterans having an evaluation by a physician is to establish that the veteran is disabled and that his/her disability is as likely as not caused by military service. Also to meet the nexus requirement.

There are two ways of establishing a nexus. The first is through an independent medical examination (IME). The second way is through an independent medical opinion (IMO). An IME consists of a visit to the doctor's office for an examination. An IMO does not require a physical exam, but requires an experienced doctor to carefully review all of the veteran's medical records and the C&P exams, then conduct an independent and thorough medical research pertaining to the conditions in the veteran's claim or appeal. In order for the doctors to write medical opinions for each disability the veteran is claiming, the veteran must submit all medical records to their doctors: diagnoses or a list of problems, nursing notes, operation reports, discharge reports, hospital admission medical exams and history reports, lab test results, x-rays, cat scan summaries, MRI, all medications, social security award letter, employer disability award letter, etc...

Veterans can submit a medical opinion letter any time during the application process. But the sooner, the better! In my case, the VA doctor who reviewed my C&P exam did not have my c-file to review all medical evidence and eventually denied me and made up a poor excuse: "The VA could not find a link between military service and medical records." So I had to file an appeal to the Board of Veterans' Appeals in Washington, DC. The judge ruled in my favor stating "the regional office and the physician did not have veteran's file when they made their decision because veteran's file has been in Washington, DC for the past five years." The law states C&P examiners must have the veteran's file at the time of the C&P exam so the examiner can review the entire file before making a decision. I won my appeal and the judge forced the regional office to back pay me five years. This was another game changer for me!

There was a research study conducted by the Institute of Medicine (IOM) to study and recommend changes in the medical evaluation and rating of veterans for the benefits provided by the VA, which compensates veterans for illnesses or injuries that occurred while in service or aggravated by service. The IOM found that there were inadequacies in the qualifications of the VA raters. The IOM research found "few VA raters have medical backgrounds. They are required to review and assess medical evidence provided by treating physicians and the VBA examining physicians to determine the percentage of disability. However the VBA does not have medical consultants or advisors to support the VA raters in decision making. Medical advisors would also improve the process of deciding what medical examinations and tests are needed to sufficiently prepare a case for rating." This is why you should file an appeal every time the VA regional office denies you.

Many times, veterans give up too quickly and think that it is final when the VA regional office denies them. I am a former employee at the VA regional office and I know the laws and regulations. I went by book, chapter, and verse when submitting all these documents mentioned in this book based on the law. The VA regional office denied me every time I filed a claim, but I won every appeal in Washington, DC. Remember, the judge has the final word and he/she will apply the law fairly to veterans!

Published medical reports in an independent medical opinion

It is very important that veterans request that their doctors submit medical reports or articles to support their claims for disability and when filing secondary condition claims. Proving a nexus between a veteran's disability and military service demands both factual and scientific evidence.

There are times when veterans do not have medical records to submit due to records being damaged or when veterans are already service-connected, usually it's a matter of whether their current disabling condition is related to their already service-connected disabilities. Secondary claims can be the difference in whether or not a veteran gets 100% permanent and total. In most cases, the secondary claims are rated higher than the original claims.

If the VA denies a veteran's claim, the VA must have an equally qualified scientist state that there is no scientific connection between the claimed condition and the service-connected conditions. Even then, the VA must accept the IMO based on the benefit of the doubt doctrine. In my opinion, veterans should make the VA have to work on your claim by submitting all kinds of evidence to support your claim because for every piece of evidence provided by private doctors, the VA will have to work that much harder to counter the leg work the veteran has put into their claim!

When I used to work at the VA regional office, I saw VA raters taking frequent coffee breaks and long lunch hours. Some would leave campus for hours going shopping and hanging out with their companions! Then when they come back to their desk, they just deny veterans benefits even when the medical evidence is in the veteran's file. Denying veterans makes the VA raters' job easy, and they get bonuses at the end of the year for every veteran they denied, based on the director's and supervisor's instructions.

DBQ form from doctor

Doctors fill out a disability benefits questionnaire (DBQ) on the veteran for each disability he/she is seeking. This can be to the veteran's advantage after the VA denies him/her. He or she can request that their doctor fill out the form in detail on behalf of the veteran. In most cases, veterans are not aware of DBQ forms, which can help in getting their benefits.

I remember taking a PTSD examination at the VA hospital that lasted about five hours. When I completed the exam, I turned it in to the clerk at the mental health department, which so happened to be the department where I was employed at the time. A few weeks later, I received a letter from the regional office stating I was denied because I did not finish and turn in the PTSD exam. So, I informed my private doctor and he gave me the same PTSD exam and completed a DBQ form, which described in detail my conditions. Then I appealed the denial letter to Washington, DC and the judge awarded me for PTSD! This was another game changer in getting my benefits.

Breaking news: the VA is constantly changing the rules and regulations. As I am writing this book, I received an e-mail alert that the VA has removed all public DBQ's from their website as of April 10, 2020. A tele-health or tele-mental health examination report will not be accepted because the veteran did not conduct the examination in person with the doctor. The VA will no longer accept DBQ's from private doctors due to fraud.

The VA claims that veterans are paying a lot of money to doctors from other states, they have not been treated in person. And when the veteran service representative (VSR) receives the paperwork, the VA finds that the DBQ does not match the medical records in the veteran's claim file. This is why it is important to know the laws and regulations.

In addition, sign up for e-mail alerts from the VA. You can also learn about VA regulations from veterans who have experience fighting the VA. It is possible that the VA may allow veterans to use DBQ's in the future with a new administration. It's unfortunate that a few bad apples in the bunch have ruined it for the veterans that go by the rules! But, keep in mind that a veteran can have a doctor write the DBQ's in letter format answering all the questions in detail. Basically, the doctor is helping the VA rating specialist to understand and complete their job. Another factor to consider, it could be a new employee working on the veteran's claim that does not have experience. So, the doctor's letter is another way to submit evidence, since the VA is no longer accepting DBQ's.

Breaking news: God is still in the business of answering prayers even for service members and veterans. I did some research and discovered a law firm that has posted on their website more than 70 Disability Benefits Questionnaire (DBQ) forms that you can download and print for your private health care provider to complete. The law firm is the National Veterans Legal Services Program. Their website is: https://www.nvlsp.org/news-and-events/press-releases/nvlsp-offers-va-disability-benefits-questionnaires

This Is A Game Changer because VA must consider All evidence you submit including DBQ because Congress have not changed the law even though VA removed DBQ forms from Its website. Please be aware you must have a different DBQ Form completed for each claim you submit. You may have to hire a lawyer to file an appeal to hold VA feet to the fire!

Disability symptoms and diagnosis

When I began to seek treatment from the VA hospital and private doctors many years ago, I did not know how to explain my pain or what I was experiencing. Unfortunately, many veterans are denied compensation because they do not know how to explain their medical condition to nurses and doctors. **You must be able to use medical terminology that nurses and doctors use.**

The best way to get a diagnosis is to research and study the medical terminology of what you are experiencing. That way, when you visit the doctor, you will have an understanding of what to tell the doctor in detail. The doctor will determine whether or not to give you a diagnosis based on the regulations. This is very important because the VA regional office will be looking in your medical records for a diagnosis from the doctor. If there is no diagnosis or a series of medical symptoms documented in your file, the regional office will automatically deny your disability claim. Documentation is the key to winning your disability! It is the veteran's responsibility to check their medical records periodically to make sure the nurses and doctors are documenting the correct symptoms, correct pain level, correct medication, and what the veteran is experiencing. This is the best way to hold the VA's feet to the fire, so to speak, because what you said or did not say can be held against you! And that is based on what is documented in your medical records.

So study and do your homework on your conditions by reading books and articles and by googling the key phrases, symptoms and what is required for the doctor to give a diagnosis. And when you visit the doctor, the key words you found are exactly what you should tell the doctor. This was a big game changer for me when I first started going to doctors for treatment. Log online and type "symptom of [disability]" and it will list symptoms in detail in medical terminology.

Veterans are encouraged to pull their VA medical records monthly to see what diagnoses the doctors have given them. This

is the easiest and quickest way to apply for disability because you have been diagnosed and are getting current treatment. Examples to research to explain to your doctor what you're experiencing:

- "symptoms of back pain"
- "symptoms of shoulder pain"
- "symptoms of sciatic nerve pain"
- "symptoms of flat feet"
- "symptoms of hypertension"
- "symptoms of sleep apnea"
- "symptoms of post-traumatic symptom disorder"

C&P examination or QTC exam

When you apply for compensation, the regional office will notify the VA hospital to schedule you a compensation & pension (C&P) exam for each disability you are applying for. **Do not downplay your conditions** when the doctor asks how you feel or what your pain level is. Tell the truth because your responses will be used to determine whether or not you are awarded disability. And it determines what rating the regional office will give you.

If you live outside a 40-mile radius of the VA hospital, then the C&P exam will be conducted by a private doctor, whose office is near your home, contracted out by the VA. From my experience, all of my success came from private doctors. When I lived near the VA hospital, I was sent to the VA hospital and they gave me the run around. The VA hospital came up with all kinds of excuses, denying me my benefits even though I had all the documents required by the VA laws and regulations set by Congress. The regional office lied and stated they denied me for an increase in PTSD for over four years because I did not turn in questions and answers to the mental health department after I took the test. In fact, my C&P exam for PTSD was conducted in the same mental health department that I worked at. I turned the paperwork in to my co-worker. As a result, I took the same PTSD exam with my private doctor and filed an appeal and won my case. The fact is that the VA regional office and the VA hospital work together to prevent most veterans from receiving their benefits. Like I stated before, if you do not know your rights, you have no rights, but if you study the VA manual, you have a leg to stand on. From my experience, it is better to live outside the VA radius in order to be scheduled for a C&P exam by private doctors. It does not work in all cases. That's why it is important to study the VA manual to dispute discrepancies.

The C&P examiner will ask questions and perform different tests based on which disability the veteran is seeking. For example, if you are seeking a back disability, a range of motion test will be performed by asking you to bend over and touch the floor. The doctor will measure how far you can bend over. The further you bend over, the less chance you have of getting a back disability from the regional office. (I bent over about 7 degrees because I had pain and stiffness in the spine and back muscles. I received 40% for back pain.) Also, it is a good idea to bring a written personal statement to give to the C&P examiner to help explain what you are experiencing in day-to-day life. This letter will be used by the examiner to write the exam report. It is always best to be prepared than to not have anything to report about your condition. The more you have, the better.

After completing the report, the C&P examiner will forward the report to the regional office. It usually takes about 45 days to get a decision from the regional office, whether or not you were awarded the disability. **If you missed your C&P exam, the regional office will automatically reduce or terminate your benefits.** If you cannot attend your C&P exam, it's best to call and reschedule.

Some other tips for your C&P exam: arrive early; study the examiner's specialty the night before the exam by Googling the examiner's profile online; be honest; bring a written list of symptoms to help refresh your memory; and bring a witness such as a spouse, relative, or friend who has witnessed what you are going through. You can also bring a medical opinion or nexus letter from a doctor that you have already submitted to the VA.

Breaking news: as I am writing this book, the VA has discontinued in-person exams as of April 2, 2020 due to the COVID-19 crisis. I assume in-person examinations will resume after COVID-19 is over.

Even during a medical crisis, the VA is slowly stripping away veterans' benefits behind the scenes under the current administration. The VA is making it harder for veterans to get the evidence they need to support their claims. As a result of VA strategy, more veterans will be denied. The current administration is making it difficult for doctors to complete reports that meet the criteria necessary for the VA to process the claims, which ultimately hurts the veterans but makes VA jobs easier!

Proving severity of conditions

Veterans should describe their pain levels in detail when visiting any doctor, whether at the VA hospital, during C&P exams, or with private doctors. If you are in pain, you should continue to complain about your pain and symptoms to your doctors to help support chronicity of your medical condition and ultimately help support your VA claim later when you apply for disability. The more severe your symptoms, the higher your rating will be. The VA representative will be looking in your c-file to see if you complained of your condition and to what extent your pain was when you reported to your doctor. The VA also looks to see how often you went to the emergency room. This can be another game changer! If there were no complaints documented in your file, you will not get a favorable decision, or no benefits at all, due to lack of medical evidence and lack of chronicity or severity. In other words, if you did not complain or your complaints were not documented in your file by a nurse or doctor, the VA will claim you are committing fraud to get benefits.

I remember a particular nurse at the VA hospital would always ask me my pain level whenever I had an appointment or went to the emergency room. I would say my pain level was 8, 9 or 10. But when I decided to obtain my medical records on a monthly basis at the VA hospital to hold their feet to the fire, I discovered that the nurse lied on my medical records and minimized my pain level, documenting that I said my pain level was a 4 instead of the 8, 9 or 10 pain level that I told her. I eventually went to patient advocacy to request a different nurse because I knew the importance of proving the chronicity of my medical condition. I knew that anything I said could be used against me or in my favor when the VA is deciding whether or not to award disabilities.

Buddy letters/lay evidence

Buddy letters are letters written by competent individuals who have had direct, first-hand knowledge of an event or injury. The letter should offer an account of what he/she witnessed or are witnessing in support of a veteran's VA disability claim. Lay statements fill gaps in a veteran's record and can be used in all disability claims to help prove his/her case. Lay evidence can also be used in individual unemployability claims.

These statements can be from a fellow soldier, spouse, co-worker, friend, pastor, supervisor, or any other credible witness. Buddy letters confirm a veteran's change in behavior after returning home from deployment. It details how the veteran's life has changed for the worse. Buddy letters constitute "lay evidence" under the law, which means "after the fact" evidence. The VA must consider a buddy letter because it is a secondary source of evidence in support of a veteran's disability claim.

Because I studied VA laws and regulations, I knew to submit a buddy letter within one year from deployment to Iraq based on VA rules and regulations. It is crucial that every veteran submit their buddy letter within the first year after deployment because this time frame is taken into consideration. Buddy letters must be filled out on a VA **form 21-4138**. It made a world of difference in receiving my rating for PTSD. This was another VA game changer for me!

Confirmed stressor letter

Veterans who are seeking disability compensation for post-traumatic stress disorder must submit a stressor statement under VA regulation. Veterans are usually denied because of a lack of a stressor statement. A stressor statement is a written, detailed account of the stressful event or series of events that triggered a veteran's PTSD. Examples of combat stressors include: grave registration, morgue assignment, accidents involving injury, combat or enemy action, witnessing mortar and rocket attacks, sexual assault, or fear of hostile military action or terrorist activity from the enemy. Medical evidence is required to establish the link between your current symptoms and the in-service stressor. My PTSD claim was another game changer for me because it is a high-value disability, meaning a veteran can get up to 100% permanent and total with no future exams!

Non-combat veterans can be diagnosed and compensated for PTSD if their stressor letter includes pulling guard duty, convoys, many hours of work, lack of sleep, heavy equipment, or having been assigned to a burned care unit. Many veterans' military experiences are considered terrifying, life threatening or stressful. Keep in mind that the relationship between stressors during military service and current problems/symptoms plays a major role in determining service-connection. Symptoms must have a clear relationship to the military stressor as described in the veteran's medical records. The veteran's application for compensation must document some of the same medical records and match the stressor letter! Most non-combat veterans qualify for depression and anxiety disorder.

How to request a DD-214 upgrade from dishonorable to honorable discharge

If you received a dishonorable discharge, you can seek an upgrade to honorable discharge, especially if it was for a bad conduct discharge. This can have a major impact on a veteran's life after military service. Once the upgrade has been approved, you will be eligible for benefits at the VA including disability compensation, education benefits, VA home loans with no down payment, social security, and access to military bases, etc.

You can apply for a discharge upgrade within 15 years after discharge. If the discharge is older than 15 years, you must apply for a change to military records by completing DD-form 293 - application for the review of discharge or dismissal from the Armed Forces of the United States. In addition to downloading the form online, DD-form 293 is also available at most DOD installations and VA regional offices. The board will upgrade your discharge only if you can prove that your discharge was inequitable or improper. You must submit evidence, such as signed statements of witnesses or copies of records that support your case. Witness statements should go in section 8 of DD-form 293. Witnesses should explain what happened and why it was an inequity or improper. Witnesses may be persons who had direct knowledge or involvement, such as your first sergeant, commander, supervisor, or chaplain.

Changes to DD-214 or other military records cannot be done through the VA. The change request must be processed through the Department of Defense (DOD), Army Review Boards Agency (ARBA).

For Army records, you must contact the Department of Defense, ARBA.

The ARBA address is:

The Army Review Board Agency (ARBA)
Attn: Client Information and Quality Assurance

251 18th Street South, Suite 385
Arlington, VA 22202-4508
Phone: 703-545-6800

Veteran may also send an e-mail to: army.arbainquiry@mail.mil.

The Army Review Boards Agency also maintains a website where veterans can complete an application for change. The website address is: http://ara.army.pentegon.mil/online-application.html.

Air Force Review Boards Agency
SAF / MRBR
550-C Street West, Suite 40
Randolph AFB, TX 78150-4742

Secretary of Navy and Marine Corps
Council of Review Boards
Attn: Naval Discharge Review Board
720 Kennon Street, S.E.
Room 309 (NDRB)
Washington Navy Yard, DC 20374-5023

Commandant of Coast Guard (CG-133)
Attn: Office of Military Personnel
U.S. Coast Guard Stop 7907
2703 Martin Luther King, Jr. Avenue, S.E.
Washington, DC 20593-7907

Recently discharged veterans

If you are a service member still on active duty or reserve status, I recommend you **go to the VA's website eBenefits and file your disabilities in batch (4-6 disability claims) 6 to 8 months before being discharged or retirement. Anything you were treated for can be claimed.** The reason to file 6 to 8 months before discharge is because it will be easier to be service-connected after deployment, since you may not have had access to doctors while deployed in combat zone. It's in your best interest to apply for disabilities as soon as possible, within one year of discharge.

Veterans who were released from the military Department of Defense's board on medical discharge with less than 100% should go to the VA medical hospital and private doctors for continued treatment. Also, keep in mind that you can apply for an increase on current disability ratings when released from the military and apply for new disabilities at the VA regional office or on the eBenefits.gov website to pursue getting 100% permanent and total. **Complete VA form 526EZ and submit copies of your DD-214 and military medical records to the VA Evidence Intake Center.** Please be aware that you will be subject to C&P exams by the VA to determine if conditions have gotten better or worse, if you do not have permanent & total status (P&T).

If you have not been going to the doctor continuously, the VA will reduce and eventually take away your disability. So my advice is **keep going to the doctor and keep submitting new evidence (nexus letters and reports) every 2 or 3 years** to get an increase and/or file an appeal until you get 100% permanent & total (P&T) status.

Different types of VA claims

You must know which classification of claims you are seeking to prevent your claims from falling through the cracks. You must do your research on your conditions before filing a claim. Study the current 38 code of federal regulations parts 3 & 4 that pertain to your claim(s). By understanding which claim you are seeking, it could speed up the process. Before submitting your claim, read and understand which claim you're seeking and the correct form because the VA is constantly changing rules and procedures. I recommend calling the VA hotline at 1-800-827-1000 or meeting with your power of attorney representative at the regional office to confirm the correct form because the VA will deny you if the wrong form is submitted.

Original claim: This is the original claim that the veteran or family member first applied for compensation on VA **form 526EZ - "disability compensation and related compensation benefits."**

New claim: Veterans can apply for new claims when eligible. If veteran is eligible and condition gets worse or cannot work or find employment due to service-related conditions, veterans can submit claims – VA **form 21-526EZ – for the** following:

A. Special monthly compensation
B. Individual unemployability
C. An increased disability evaluation

Reopened claim: Veterans can reopen VA claims with new and material evidence the VA hadn't considered in the original claim. If you were previously denied, you will need to submit new and material evidence showing why service connection is warranted. Veteran must submit VA **form 20-0995 - "decision review request: supplemental claim"** along with both new and material evidence with the application. New and material evidence includes medical tests or a doctor's evaluation. To reopen a claim, a medical condition must have changed for the worse. A decision from the regional office usually takes 4 to 5 months.

Veterans can request a senior level officer at the regional office to take another look at their claim if veteran was previously denied by the regional office. You must file a VA **form 20-0996 - "higher-level review claim"** and send it to the Evidence Intake Center. A decision review officer at the regional office will look to see if previously denied claims can be changed based on any errors made by the staff. Please note that **no new evidence can be submitted,** so please make sure you include all the evidence and do not expect any more medical evidence from doctors. The decision review officer (DRO) at the regional office will determine whether the decision can be changed based on a difference of opinion or errors.

Secondary claim: A service-connected disability causes a new disability as a result or was worsened. Veteran must submit VA form 526EZ.

Fully developed claim: This program is designed for veterans who have all documents written for the VA to expedite or process the claim in a quick manner by submitting VA form 526EZ. Veteran is stating that there is no additional evidence, which enables the VA to make a decision more quickly. But if new evidence comes up later on, the VA will place the claim in the standard claim process. Veteran must submit to VA the service treatment and personnel records to speed up the process of getting a decision as soon as possible.

Standard claim process: Under standard claim process, the VA has more responsibility to assist the veteran in obtaining the information needed to support the veteran's claim. The veteran is able to submit additional evidence for up to one year after he/she has filed their claim. To apply for standard claim process, check the box under item 1 at the top of VA form 21-526EZ.

The best time to apply for VA disability

If you are a service member in the reserve, you should seek medical treatment from your doctor when your unit is activated. By doing so, you will have all your physical exams done before leaving the military. I also recommend service members who are on active duty to go to sick call and tell the doctor in detail any illnesses or injuries you have. **Get everything documented. Make sure you get a copy of your military records for yourself before you out process.** Congress has written a law known as "presumptive disability." It basically says that **a condition is presumptive and does not require a medical opinion from a doctor but veteran must have all elements of condition met.**

The VA presumes that specific disabilities diagnosed in certain veterans were caused by their military service. The VA does this because of the unique circumstances of military service. If a veteran is diagnosed with one of the following conditions in one of the following groups, the VA presumes that the circumstances of the veteran's service caused the condition, and disability compensation can be awarded. There are several conditions that are presumed to be caused by military service. Gulf War veterans who have undiagnosed illnesses who served in the Southwest Asia theater of operations during the Gulf War with "presumed conditions" who had the following conditions for 6 months or more include: chronic fatigue syndrome, fibromyalgia, irritable bowel syndrome, skin condition, headaches, muscle pain, joint pain, neurological symptoms, respiratory symptoms, sleep disturbance, cardiovascular symptoms, weight loss, menstrual disorders, or any diagnosed or undiagnosed illness that the secretary of veterans affairs determines warrants a presumption of service connection.

It's easier to prove your service-connected disability when you apply for disability later with the VA regional office if you were treated for conditions while on active duty and it was documented in your military medical records. The first thing the regional office will look for is whether or not you went to sick call and complained of your pain while you were in the military. So think ahead. You will not always be young and in top shape! We all get old, and our bodies will eventually give out on us. So take advantage of my experience as a veteran who has worked the system, knows the process, knows the law, and has won every appeal in Washington, DC. A smart person will heed to good advice and plan for the future.

VA claims effective date

When veterans get awarded disability, excitement comes but many times veterans overlook the effective date. The VA may have shortchanged them out of hundreds of thousands of dollars. It is very important that you verify you receive the correct amount of back pay if awarded disability or increase.

The VA has two rules when it comes to back pay and effective dates. The first is that the date the VA received the application for benefits is the effective date, not the date you faxed or mailed the application. Second, the effective date occurs the date the veteran qualifies for disability. An example would be if you apply for sleep apnea expecting a 50% rating, but the regulations state you must have a c-pap machine to qualify for a 50% rating. So the veteran gets the sleep machine about a year later. As a result of not having the c-pap machine at the time of submitting the application for sleep apnea, the VA will assign an effective date a year later, on the day you received the c-pap machine, meaning the veteran would miss out on thousands of dollars simply because veteran did not know this rule.

To sum it up, I recommend keeping your original copies with a dated stamp on the front of the VA application for disability in case you have to appeal later to get your back pay. If you feel you did not receive all of your back pay, I recommend waiting until you receive your back pay money before filing an appeal because it will slow down the process and you won't receive anything!

Veterans can file an appeal on incorrect effective date in one of the following ways:

1. https://va.gov
2. https://eBenefits.gov

3. Mail completed VA form to:

Board of Veterans' Appeals
Attention: Intake Center
P.O. box 5229
Janesville, Wisconsin 53547-5235
fax #: 1-844-678-8979

4. An accredited representative or agent
5. Veteran can bring their application to nearest VA regional office near their home residence. Get a stamped copy for your records.

Track status of VA claims
by calling VA at 1-800-827-1000

It is very important to follow up with the VA on a regular basis after you have turned in your application for benefits. You must take ownership of your claim. I recommend calling the VA every week. By doing so, you send a message to the VA that you are not going to allow them to put your claim on the back of the shelf and forget about you. I know from experience that the VA will not process claims unless they are forced to do so!

A VA scandal came out a few years ago with evidence of shredding veterans' applications for benefits to make their workload appear outstanding in order to get Christmas bonuses at the end of the year. My claim for TDIU sat in the VA file room for four years and I had to file a CUE claim through an appeal at the Board of Veterans' Affairs (BVA). The judge in DC forced the VA regional office to process my TDIU claim. Two days later, the director was forced to approve my TDIU and a supervisor was forced to call me informing me I have been approved for TDIU. The regional office was forced to back pay me four years at the 100% TDIU rate = $3,000 × 48 months!

How to apply for an increase in disability ratings

There are two ways to get an increase in your disability ratings. This should be the goal of all veterans. Most veterans are not aware that if they don't pursue increases until veteran reaches permanent and total, the VA will reduce or take away the veteran's disability. This is why the VA sends veterans on C&P exams every two or three years: to see if the condition has gotten better or worse. The veteran's condition and disability rating can remain the same.

Under no condition should you accept the VA keeping your disability rating the same because the VA will chip away and reduce your disability rating later on if you have stopped going to doctors' appointments or have stopped taking medication. Tip: to obtain disability and maintain disability from the VA and social security, you must keep going to the doctor and keep submitting paperwork proving your conditions have gotten worse. It is very important that you continue to get ongoing treatment for your service-connected disability in order to get an increase every three years until you have obtained 100% permanent and total status.

By getting ongoing treatment and rating increases, you prevent the VA from reducing or taking away your benefits. The best way to do this is to complain continuously to your doctors about chronic pain that interferes with your daily activities. The VA regional office looks for consistency in veterans getting treatment. You must have faith and trust the process!

I fought the VA for 21 years by continuing to make my doctors' appointments, taking medication, and submitting updated nexus letters from my doctors that my condition has gotten worse. Finally, I met the rating protection of permanent and total. The law states in the VA rules and regulations that if a veteran has had a disability rating for 20 years, an assignment rating must be permanent and total. In addition, I don't have to complete any more future exams, which is stated in my VA award letter. I have put in my time fighting the VA.

Another game changer is when veterans apply for appeals. The longer it takes for an appeal to go to a judge in Washington DC, the better, because all that time counts towards your 20 years to get rating protection called permanent and total disability. In some cases, veterans are awarded permanent and total sooner, depending on who is working on the veteran's file.

Unfortunately for me, I was given a bad hand to work with. But I had faith in God I knew that God would have the final word. I kept fighting and kept getting older. And after 10, 15 years, I looked back and I made up my mind: I've come too far to give up. God did not bring me this far to leave me even when I was homeless and the VA kept denying me of my benefits. I kept reading God's word to find relief and comfort after being on the battlefield in Iraq and returning home to the VA regional office giving me more hell and stress, denying me benefits the government promised when I gave my life through service to my country.

I read in God's word "No man shall be able to stand before you all the days of your life, as I was with Moses, so I will be with you. I will not leave you nor forsake you. Be strong and courageous that you may observe to do according to all the law. This book of the law shall not depart from your mouth, but you shall meditate in the bible day and night according to what is written in it. And then you will make your way prosperous, and then you shall have good success. Do not be afraid or dismayed, for the Lord your God is with you wherever you go" – Joshua 1:5-9.

A lot of time, I see too often veterans giving up too quickly because they didn't get the results they were seeking at the VA regional office. In my case, I knew the rules and regulations and submitted all documents required under the law, and still the VA continued to deny me every time I was called in for C&P exams. But I appealed the VA regional office decision letters every time to the Board of Veterans' Appeals in Washington DC and I got increases from the judge. When I first applied for compensation, I put in claims for several conditions all at the same time and stuck with those conditions without having to apply for more later, which I had an option to do but applying for too many conditions would have set me back. The VA would think I was holding up their workload and other veterans from getting their claims processed.

There are two ways veterans can get increases. I got my increases through appeals. Every time the VA regional office denied me or let my rating remain the same, I filed an appeal and got an increase every time! There are two ways to receive an increase to an existing disability:

1. Veteran must have medical proof that his/her condition has gotten worse. This can be from either the VA doctor or a private doctor. Tip: I have had great success from private doctors, which is a game changer! You can file an increase request using the eBenefits website or by completing VA form 21-526EZ. And if you are being treated by a private doctor, you must complete VA form 21-42, which authorizes your private doctor to share information with the VA. Submit VA form 21-526EZ and other documents for increase to:

   Department of Veterans Affairs
   Claims Intake Center
   P.O. box 4444
   Janesville, Wisconsin 53547-4444
   Fax #: 1-844-531-7818

2. You can appeal the VA regional office every time the VA requests you for a C&P exam. Once you receive the VA regional office's decision letter, always challenge it and hire an attorney to file your appeals because the VA changed the rules of the game February 19, 2019. If the VA regional office decides to keep you at the same rating, do not settle because you have just added more time to fight the VA when that time could have gone towards the appeals judge who will give you the correct rating and correct effective date. Which will be less time the regional office can chip away your VA rating. When God has the final word, there's nothing the regional office can do about it. Trust me. I know from experience!

Total disability based on individual unemployability (TDIU) = IU

TDIU is a benefit the VA awards veterans who are unable to work due to their service-connected disability(s) to obtain disability compensation equal to 100% rating. Congress has written into VA law policy that veterans who are not able to secure and maintain substantially gainful employment due to service-connected disabilities shall be rated totally disabled. 38 c.f.r. 4.16 (b). Veterans Affairs defines unemployability as follows [40 fr 42536, Sept. 15, 1975, as amended at 43 fr 45349, Oct. 2, 1978]:

"A veteran may be considered as unemployable upon termination of employment which was provided because disability, or in which special consideration was given on account of the same, when it is satisfactorily shown that he or she is unable to secure further employment [...] however, consideration is to be given to the circumstances of employment was only occasional, intermittent, try out or unsuccessful, or eventually terminated on account of the disability, present unemployability may be attributed to the static disability."

The VA will grant 100% TDIU disability rating based on individual unemployability (IU) when a veteran cannot obtain or keep employment due to service-connected disabilities. The VA requires a nexus letter from the veteran's doctor stating he/she is no longer able to work due to service-connected disability. This was another game changer for me after my job put me on disability. I was 90% - 70% PTSD, 50% sleep apnea, 40% back pain - and later I applied for TDIU based on my combined ratings. The regional office never processed my claim. Four years later, I had to file a clear unmistakable error to the judge in DC and won my case. The judge awarded me 90% TDIU, which became permanent five years later after I requested permanent and total status! Even though I am 90%, the VA pays me at 100% rate because my job put me on disability due to my service-connected disability.

I did not know I qualified for TDIU after all my ratings increased to 90%. The regional office did not bring it to my attention or send me the TDIU application, which pays veterans at the 100% rate. Many times, veterans apply for this benefit too early in the game and get denied by the regional office because they did not meet the rating criteria of one disability at 60% or multiple disabilities with an overall rating of 70%, with one of those disabilities rated at 40%. So, my recommendation is to get your rating(s) as high as you can, then apply for disability from your job and apply for social security the same day. Your employer will give you a code to apply for social security.

Wait until you have received a disability award letter from your job and social security, then apply for TDIU with the VA and submit proof from two agencies that you are disabled, which will make your case strong for TDIU. The regional office will likely deny you as usual, but file an appeal and submit all medical records, medical opinion from doctors, disability award letters from social security, and your employer disability award letter to your attorney who will then file a TDIU appeal to the VA Board of Veterans Appeals in Washington, DC. You will then win your TDIU claim in the appeal court in DC with a judge and back pay! This is the secret to winning your TDIU claim.

When a veteran's combined multiple disabilities rating is less than 100%, the VA will pay the veteran the same amount as a veteran who receives 100%. For example, if a veteran has one disability at 60%, and a doctor has said he/she can no longer work due to that service-connected disability, a 60% rating pays about $1,113.86 a month. But if the veteran is approved for TDIU, the pay goes up to $3,106 a month, which is a game changer. **It's highly recommended that veterans hire an attorney to file a TDIU claim ASAP after the veteran's private doctor has written an independent nexus letter stating veteran can no longer work due to their military service-connected disabilities**. The attorney will not charge you upfront fees but will get a small portion of your back pay when you get awarded disability.

Many veterans miss out on hundreds of thousands of dollars because they failed to file for TDIU. Simply because they did not know about the claim! It is hard to get 100% P&T if you are 70%, 80%, or 90%. That's why TDIU is a game changer. It is a backdoor to getting paid at the 100% rate, which pays $3,100 monthly for a veteran ranging from 70%-90% with individual unemployability.

TDIU claims are difficult and complex. Therefore, **it is best to hire a lawyer to file your TDIU claim**. The regional office may not process your claim, hoping you forget about it, which happened to me. I waited four years and the regional office thought I had forgot until I filed a CUE claim for refusing to process my TDIU claim. The regional office is known to deny veterans' claim for TDIU for no reason.

Veterans should go to Kinkos to make copies of all their medical records and doctors' letters to submit to everyone involved in the process of getting their disability. Include copies for veteran's doctors, your employer, the VA, and social security. Every time you get an award letter from an agency, make copies and submit them to everyone I just listed above because each agency cross references each other. Every agency should have the same medical records, etc... Leave no stone untouched because a missing letter or missing medical record could be the difference in getting your disability approved or not. I recall spending $75 dollars for copies of my medical records at Kinkos because I had about 700 pages of VA medical records and private doctors' medical records from over 15 years of going to several doctors' offices.

Veterans should submit a well-documented evidence claim to better his/her chances of being approved for TDIU without having to go the appeals route. I recommend you submit everything you have in regards to medical records. This includes: social security award letter, job disability award letter, VA award letters, VA medical records, private hospital medical records, medical records from private doctors, lay evidence or statements from spouse or fellow soldier who knows your conditions, independent medical opinions or nexus letters from private doctors stating veteran is not capable of working due to military service-connected disability(s), vocational assessments, and statements from former employers including employers who terminated veteran and potential employers who rejected veteran's application because of service-connected disability(s). Be sure to get letters from these employers, whether it was for termination or the employer approved disability. Also, get an award letter from social security if you are on SSDI or receiving SSI to prove you are disabled due to unemployability to make a case strong for VA's TDIU claim.

National Guard and Reservists are eligible to apply for individual unemployability (IU) if they were activated by the federal government. But they are not eligible if their state government activated their unit.

Most veterans awarded TDIU or IU have a combination of mental and physical disabilities. Veterans with post-traumatic stress disorder (PTSD) are usually granted TDIU at an earlier age because of the effects of the mental illness, like myself who is a Gulf War veteran and Iraq combat veteran, which is coded on my DD-214. For more information on how to file PTSD, visit the VA website: **https://www.va.gov/disability/ eligibility/PTSD/**.

In order to be eligible for IU or TDIU, a veteran must meet the following criteria:

1. A combination of multiple disabilities rated 70% overall or higher (with at least one of those disabilities being rated at 40% or higher)
2. A single disability rating of at least 60% or higher and veteran is mentally unable to work (example: PTSD 60% or higher)

To apply for total disability individual unemployability (TDIU) or individual unemployability (IU), you must complete and submit the following 2 forms along with all medical records:

- **VA form 21-4192 - a request for employment information in connection with claim for disability benefits - sent to current and former employers.**
- **VA form 21-526EZ application for disability and related compensation benefits (individual unemployability).**

Complete both forms and mail or fax to the VA Evidence Intake Center:

Department of Veterans' Affairs
Claims Intake Center
P.O. box 4444
Janesville, Wisconsin 53547-4444
Fax #: 1-844-531-7818

TDIU is not permanent and the veteran is subject to C&P exams every two years for rating reductions to determine if he/she has been working or if the condition has gotten better. On the other hand, if conditions have gotten worse, with a private doctor's independent medical opinion, the veteran can request to be awarded permanent and total status (P&T). The VA will conduct audits from social security to see if the veteran has been working every year up to five years from the last audit. If the veteran has been working, the VA will take away TDIU.

Veterans must complete and submit VA form 526EZ - application for disability compensation and related compensation benefits seeking "permanent & total for each issue or disability." Mail or fax VA form 526EZ to the VA Evidence Intake Center along with a private doctor's independent medical opinion.

On the form, you must list the issues or conditions you are seeking to be permanent. The VA will evaluate your entire file and come up with reasons not to grant you "permanent and total status." There's a possibility the VA will reduce ratings if you have stopped going to the doctor. So a word of precaution: **before you apply for P&T status, make sure you're continuing to go to all doctor's appointments for every disability you have and visiting emergency rooms if necessary because this is your only defense to prevent the VA from reducing your disability rating. Ongoing treatment, diagnoses, and a list of medications you're taking with an updated private doctor's independent medical opinion letter stating your issue or condition has gotten worse or continues to get** worse is the only way to get permanent and total status. Receiving ongoing treatment for 20 years will entitle the veteran to the 20-year protection law "permanent and total" status.

Now, the VA will play games and do their best to trip you up and reduce your rating! You do not have control over what the VA regional office does! The regional office is doing their job to prevent and make it hard for veterans to get their benefits. But you do have control over what you as a veteran can do. That's why I have written this book: to show veterans their rights and how to play and beat the VA regional office at its own game! That is why it is important to know and understand the VA laws, including parts of the current 38 code of federal regulations parts 3 & 4 that pertain to each of your claim(s).

As I mentioned before, in my case, I had to file a clear unmistakable error (CUE) claim against the VA regional office because they did not process my TDIU claim. In order to put in a clear unmistakable error claim, you must know and prove which law the VA regional office violated in their decision making. In other situations, you may have to file an appeal to the Board of Veterans' Appeals in DC. Once you have obtained permanent & total status with TDIU, the VA will no longer conduct future exams, which is the ultimate prize!

Please be advised, the VA regional office will not tell you this. The VA regional office is supposed to take into consideration TDIU when reviewing a veteran's file to see if he/she qualifies for unemployability and issue the TDIU form. However, in my case, the VA regional office did not consider me for TDIU. When I appealed each of my four claims that were denied by the regional office to the Board of Veterans' Appeals in DC, the judge mailed me the TDIU application. Then the judge mailed the completed form to the regional office. Four years went by and the regional office still did not process my claim for TDIU. But the regional office did send a proposal letter to reduce my PTSD from 50% to 10%, which would have made me not eligible for TDIU. At that point, I was mad as hell and filed a CUE claim against the regional office – a 3 page letter to the judge in DC through appeal – because the regional office purposely and strategically did not process my TDIU claim.

A few months later, I received a letter from the judge ruling the CUE claim in my favor, which affected all four of my original claims/appeals, and I won all four appeals. The judge forced the regional office to back pay me for four years of TDIU. It pays to know your rights and know the VA rules and regulations. It is a shame and disgrace before God how the VA treated me and denied me the benefits I earned.

What to do if the regional office denies your TDIU claim

If a veteran gets a denied letter from the regional office, it is not over. Like I always say, "Never accept a "no" from the VA. Never quit, never give up. Every day God wakes you up is another chance to get it right. It ain't over until God says so!"

Veterans have 2 options depending on the date of the denied letter for TDIU. If it is less than 12 months, then you should file an appeal to keep the original date for back pay later when you are awarded TDIU. The second option would be if 12 months have passed since the denial date for TDIU, then you will have to reapply by simply completing another TDIU application, sign it with the current date, and resubmit the application. One of these two options should eventually get you TDIU if you read my book and follow all directions!

1. Less than 12 months since being denied for TDIU: complete VA **form 10182 decision review request: board appeal (notice of disagreement)**. Submit appeal to address below:

    Board of Veterans' Appeals
    Attention: Intake Center
    P.O. box 5229
    Janesville, Wisconsin 53547-5235
    fax #: 1-844-678-8979

2. **Re-apply** if it has been more than 12 months since being denied for TDIU. The veteran will have to complete a new TDIU application, sign it with the current date, and resubmit the application to the following address below:

Department of Veteran Affairs
Claims Intake Center
P.O. box 5235
Janesville, Wisconsin 53547-5235
fax #: 1-844-531-7818

VA TDIU unemployability (TDIU) and social security benefits

The social security administration (SSA) administers benefit programs, including social security retirement, disability benefits, and Medicare. Veterans may be entitled to social security work credits for active service performed after September 15, 1940. Call the social security office at 800-772-1213. Veterans can apply for social security by calling 800-772-1213, or by going online to: **www.ssa.gov/.** The website lists all the documents you will need to apply for social security.

Veterans should apply for social security benefits at the same time their job places them on disability. Veterans are eligible to **apply for social security benefits as soon as their employer has placed them on disability by completing VA form 21-8940 – application for increased compensation based on unemployability.** The veteran's private doctor must write an independent medical opinion letter stating reasons why he/she can no longer work due to their service-connected disabilities or other disabilities. Also, remember that in section I of the application, which asks about disability and medical treatment, your answer must be that your service-connected disabilities are the reason you are unable to work.

If there are non-service-connected disabilities involved, then the veteran must get a statement from their doctor as to why the non-service-connected disabilities are not a factor in the veteran being unable to work. It very important to provide names of doctors treating the veteran's service-connected disabilities and how often (monthly, weekly, every other week, etc.) instead of giving specific dates. Also, submit all diagnoses that the VA has not awarded disabilities for because social security is a different agency and will consider all medical records. The nexus letter from a doctor should include a description of the status of existing medical conditions, disease or injury, evaluation of veteran's ability or inability to work, diagnosis, and prognosis of veteran's medical condition.

If a veteran is working for the federal government, he/she may be eligible for disability retirement from a federal job also. You will have to apply for disability through the human resources office at your job. Turn in all copies of medical records, doctors' letters placing veteran on medical leave, medication, medical devices you are using such as a back brace, knee brace, cane, or wheelchair, and submit a private doctor's independent medical opinion nexus letter to your employer's human resources. Once the human resources office receives all documents, they will give you a code to log on to the social security website to apply for benefits the same day. You should receive an award letter from your job stating you have been approved for disability from your job before the social security hearing because it takes longer for social security to approve, approximately two years.

Please submit all copies of letters and medical records to your social security lawyer to help build your case for social security. Social security usually denies people the first time and second time when you request reconsideration. I recommend you skip over the reconsideration request and just hire a social security lawyer the first time when you are denied to speed up the process. Once you go to your social security hearing with your lawyer, it takes about 60 days to start receiving your social check.

Once you have received a disability award letter from your job and a social security award letter stating you have been approved for disability, submit all copies of disability letters to the VA to support your claim for TDIU. This will strengthen your TDIU/IU claim because it shows that two different agencies have approved you for disability. I recommend submitting all medical records with diagnoses and doctors' nexus letters to each agency in which you are seeking benefits to make your case stronger.

I also recommend you hire a lawyer when applying for TDIU or an individual unemployability claim with the VA because the VA is known to make things difficult and tricky, especially when you are applying for individual unemployability because it pays at 100% rate, approximately $3,000 a month for a single veteran. (The attorneys will not charge upfront fees but receive a small portion of back payment from social security and your individual unemployability claim.)

Please be advised, a lot of veterans apply for TDIU too early and tip the VA as to what the veteran's ultimate goal is. I recommend once you have met eligibility for TDIU such as PTSD, depression and anxiety, or other disability, then apply. It's best to wait until you have a high rating before applying for TDIU: 60% for single disability or several disabilities or 70% combined rating with one disability at 40%. When the dust settles, you should be getting disability checks from your employer if eligible, VA disability, and social security - 3 disability checks each month for life.

Veterans have the option of getting Medicare with social security. I elected part A, which is free, because I pay monthly premiums with Blue Cross Blue Shield and I get free treatment at the VA medical center. For more information on Medicare through social security, please call 800-633-4227 or visit their website at: medicare.gov. You will be given the option once you have been approved for social security.

VA compensation & pension exams or QTC exams

Once a veteran has obtained permanent and total status, he/she will no longer have to be called in every two years to prove his/her disability! It took me 21 years of going to the doctor to keep my benefits and keep my rating increasing. Any time you stop going to the doctor, you have just given the VA permission to reduce and take away your benefits. And it is legal for the VA to strip away your benefits.

When veterans are called in for C&P exams, they should research the C&P examiner's background the day before the exam to see if they are qualified to conduct the exam. The regional office is known to use non-professionals who are not qualified due to high demands and costs. Some examiners are general practitioners while others are board certified. If the examiner is a general practitioner and you were denied a claim, this would be grounds to appeal your case to the Board of Veterans' Appeals (BVA) in Washington, DC.

A lot of veterans are not aware that they can request a copy of their C&P exam to see what the examiner wrote. This information can be used to file appeals. So it's the veteran's job to find loopholes in the system and prove that the regional office did not follow regulations, manuals, and case law based upon the laws written by Congress. This is grounds to file a clear unmistakable error (CUE) claim against the regional office or file an appeal to the board in DC with a judge.

The VA manual m21 part 4 mandates the regional office must provide the veteran with a thorough and complete C&P examination by reviewing his/her entire c-file. I had to appeal every two or three years when I was called in for C&P exams. The regional office always denied me, so I learned the laws that Congress had written so that I could use them in my favor when fighting the regional office. I just repeated the above steps until I was finally awarded permanent and total (P&T) status based on the 20-year protection law. Never accept a denied claim or the VA keeping your rating the same since your last C&P exam. Never give up! Now that you have my play-by-play book, let it be a game changer!

Social security follow-ups - **keep going to the doctor and keep updated letters from doctors to submit if requested!** SSA sends an employment survey every year to the address on file asking if a veteran has worked on a job in the last 12 months. In addition, SSA will send you a disability update report every 2, 3, 5, or 7 years depending on whether or not SSA believes your condition will improve or not. These follow-up reports are sent until the person reaches 63 years of age when disability is classified as retirement. They ask questions like, have you worked for someone or been self-employed, have you attended school or a work training program since the last follow-up, has your doctor told you that you cannot work or are you able to go back to work, describe your health - better, same, worse, have you gone to a doctor for treatment, are you taking medication, list what conditions you have been treated for, etc. When applying for social security disability, veterans must complete either of the following two documents to obtain copies of their medical records from the VA:

1. **VA form 10-5345: request for and authorization to release medical records or health information. This form gives social security permission to get your records from the VA.**
2. VA **form 10-5345a: individual request for a copy of own health information**. The veteran completes this form if he/she is personally requesting medical information from the VA to include in the application for social security disability benefits. This same form can be used when applying for private life insurance.

It is very important to make copies of service records, service medical records, VA medical records, and private doctors' medical records and letters. Submit all copies of records to every agency you are seeking disability from, your VA lawyer, social security lawyer, and human resources at your job if you are employed.

You can obtain a copy of your claims folder and VA medical records by submitting a written FOIA (freedom of information act) request to the VA by mail and or fax to:

Department of Veteran Affairs
Evidence Claims Intake Center
P.O. box 5235
Janesville, Wisconsin 53547-5235
fax #: 1-844-531-7818

"I am requesting a copy of my entire claims folder, including all military personal records, service treatment records, rating decisions, rating code sheets, compensation and pension exams from the VA and/or third party contractors such as LHI and QTC and any other information in my electronic claims folder not listed above."

How to get social security as a private citizen

The social security administration (SSA) administers benefit programs, including social security retirement, disability benefits, and Medicare. You may be entitled to social security as a private citizen. You may contact the security office at 800-772-1213 or apply online at: **www.ssa. gov/.** You will also have options to apply for disability and Medicare benefits on the social security website. The website lists all documents you will need to apply for social security.

There are several factors that indicate you may have a strong social security disability case. First, if you are 50 years or older, the rules are a little easier for you. Second, if you have had a steady work history most of your life. Third, if you get regular treatment for your conditions that prevent you from working. Fourth, if your daily activities are limited by conditions you have. Fifth, if you are compliant with your doctors' orders. Have you received medical treatment without gaps in treatment? Next, do you have a diagnosis from your doctor for your conditions saying that you do have the particular condition in which you are seeking disability? Have your medical condition translated into work capacity limitation by having your doctor fill out a functional capacity evaluation or complete a narrative report that addresses your limitations that are caused by your medical condition(s) and how it impacts your work.

A judge will be looking for certain evidence in your medical records, including objective medical evidence such as MRI, CT scans, and EMG tests to back up your claim. The judge will see if you're on heavy medications with serious side effects. If you have high blood pressure, the judge will look to see if your doctor prescribed a high blood pressure device to keep track of your blood pressure. Also, judges look for surgeries, physical therapy and whether you have been taking heavy doses of medication or were admitted into an inpatient mental healthcare facility for suicide attempts. The judge will also look in your medical records to see if you submitted letters from co-workers, supervisors, or human resources.

You may qualify for a mental disorder or a physical disorder. Some mental disorders include: bipolar disorder, depression, anxiety disorder, post-traumatic disorder. You will need to see a psychologist and a psychiatrist. Make sure you are taking your medications and keeping your doctors informed if you need to switch medications due to side effects. Tell your doctor everything, including how your conditions have affected your daily activities such as not being able to climb up stairs, do chores around the house, drive, cook, and take baths by yourself.

When you go to the hearing, the social security office will have a representative to show the judge some jobs that you may qualify for even with your mental or physical disorders.

The best way to win your social security case is to have both physical disorders and mental disorders. For example, consider a strong back injury MRI showing spinal cord or herniated disc. There is evidence that the pain radiates in both legs. Physical therapy and shots did not work. Surgery took place and it did not work. Now you are on pain management medications. It has caused you depression, so you see a mental health doctor and are now taking antidepressants. Make sure you see doctors who work in your best interest and are willing and able to fill out reports and letters for you to submit to your social security lawyer for the hearing! Also, submit any family medical leave documents, especially if it states you're not able to come back to work. FML is an employee record, not medical records, but the judge will see if you have been at a job for a long time. The judge will also see that you have a decline in work attendance.

You must study what disability you're experiencing that is similar to other veterans. You must go to the doctor frequently and get a diagnosis in your medical records. You can also request that your doctor type a nexus or independent medical opinion letter stating you are disabled and putting you on bedrest. Submit letters to your employer from your doctors recommending you go on sick leave for a week or two. Keep all original letters and submit copies. I would go to Kinkos and print colored copies. And if you're seeking disability from your employer, submit everything including medical records and letters from doctors stating you're no longer able to work.

Be aware that sometimes employers give an employee a hard time out of retaliation that the supervisor or co-workers will have to do your work until your disability is approved. So be careful when dealing with an employer during this process! The employer will have to submit paperwork stating how many days you have taken off from work in regard to your disability. The employer will also calculate how much they will have to pay you if approved for social security disability.

You will have the option to continue your health insurance while on leave and waiting for approval. I recommend keeping your health insurance because it will help pay your medical bills. So when you visit your doctor, you only pay for co-pays around $30 or $40. It's very important to keep your health insurance to prevent unexpected medical bills when you get sick and have to go to the emergency room.

Once you receive a letter from social security, you can determine if you've been approved. You can also speed up the payment process by contacting social security within five business days or by visiting the local office. You can locate the closest SSA office by visiting their website: https://secure.ssa.gov/icon/main.jsp. Bring a picture ID and the award letter with you. Ask the representative when the payments will be released to you because you need to pay bills.

Social security will look at whether or not your doctor prescribed your assistive devices, which will be in your favor instead of you buying devices at a store. So ask your doctor to put in a prescription for you to use prosthetics equipment such as a back brace, knee brace, cane, or wheelchair. When you go to your hearing, make sure you are wearing your devices. The judge is looking to see if you are exaggerating your conditions and you could be denied. So make sure it's documented in your record that the doctor ordered your medical devices!

The judge will ask you to describe your daily activities. Examples would be: you don't cook like you used to and now use the microwave because it's too painful to stand up for long periods of time. This shows your limitations in daily activities. If you drive, tell the judge you can't drive more than 10 minutes from the house, otherwise you have to get out of the car because of back pain and sciatica nerve pain in both legs. You're basically describing how your daily activities have changed with different limitations.

Social security wants to know if you're taking medications, how often, and the dosage level. Keep in mind, if you're approved for social security, they will periodically check up on you to see if you're continuing to visit doctors' offices and ordering your medication. Judges pay close attention to what medication you're taking because it helps judges determine very quickly whether or not your medical condition is chronic but manageable or severe and disabling. Make sure it is documented in your medical records that your doctor prescribed the medication instead of you going to Walgreens to purchase meds.

If the judge sees that your doctor is constantly changing your medications because of side effects, it shows that the doctor does not have your condition under control, which likely limits your daily activities, and you will have a high chance of winning your case. Like with the VA, your condition could improve, meaning social security could strip away your disability. So keep going to the doctor and keep your letters updated from your doctors and submit them when social security requests them. In my opinion, it is a lifestyle when you become disabled. Your disability will be with you until you die!

Social security disability listings:

- Musculoskeletal problems including back injuries
- Cardiovascular conditions including heart failure or coronary artery disease
- Senses and speech issues, including vision and hearing loss
- Respiratory illnesses including COPD or asthma
- Neurological disorders including MS, cerebral palsy, Parkinson's disease, or epilepsy

- Mental disorders including depression, anxiety, post-traumatic stress disorder, autism, or intellectual disorder
- Immune system disorders including HIV/aids, lupus, and rheumatoid arthritis
- Various syndromes including skin disorders such as dermatitis
- Digestive tract problems including liver disease or IBD
- Kidney disease and genitourinary problems
- Cancer, and the impact of standard treatments can be disabling
- Hematological disorders including hemolytic anemias and disorders of bone marrow failure

Social security disability listings that qualify for expedited approval with confirmed diagnosis from doctor and medical treatment records:

- Acute leukemia
- Lou Gehrig's disease (ALS)
- Stage IV breast cancer
- Gallbladder cancer
- Early-onset Alzheimer's disease
- Small cell lung cancer
- Hepatocellular carcinoma
- Pancreatic cancer
- Anaplastic thyroid carcinoma

Social security survivor beneficiaries

Family members of a deceased loved one who was receiving social security at the time of death are entitled to social security benefits. Family members include spouse, child, or parent. The deceased person must have worked long enough to receive benefits. There are times when a widow or widower can become disabled; they receive what is called widow's benefits. The widow or widower must have become disabled within seven years of their spouse's death. Second, they must be age 50-60. Third, they must meet social security's definition of disability, which says they must be disabled and unable to perform either their past work or any other kind of work as a result of a severe mental or physical impairment that is expected to last or has lasted for twelve months or is expected to result in death.

Social security eliminates the disability requirement once a survivor is over age 60. In order to receive survivor benefits, the widow or widower has to be married to the deceased person. If the widow or widower was working, they would get the highest payment between the deceased person compared to the widow or widower's pay. When a loved one dies, you should **contact the social security office at 800-772-1213 to report a death and apply for benefits**. Certain family members are eligible to receive monthly benefits, including:

- A widow or widower age 60 or older (age 50 or older if disabled)
- A surviving divorced spouse under certain situations
- A widow or widower at any age who is caring for the deceased's child who is under age sixteen or disabled and getting benefits on their record.
- An unmarried child of the deceased who is:
  A. Younger than age 18 (or up to age 19 if he or she is a full-time student in an elementary or secondary school); or
  B. Age 18 or older with a disability that began before age 22.

VA pension and fiduciary services

VA aid and attendance or housebound benefits provide monthly payments in addition to the amount of a monthly VA pension for qualified veterans and their survivors. Examples include a veteran that needs help with daily activities or is housebound may qualify for this benefit. If a veteran gets a VA pension and spends most of their time at home due to a permanent disability, he/she may be eligible for either aid and attendance or housebound allowance. Please be aware that a veteran cannot get both aid and attendance and housebound allowance at the same time! If a veteran receives a VA pension and meets at least one of the requirements listed below, he/she may be eligible for this benefit. At least one of these must exist below:

1. Veteran needs another person to help them perform daily activities such as feeding, bathing, and dressing,
2. Veteran is a patient in a nursing home due to loss of mental or physical abilities related to a disability
3. Veteran eyesight is limited
4. Veteran has to stay in bed due to illnesses

Veteran can apply for aid and attendance or housebound benefits by completing VA form 21-2680 - examination for housebound status or permanent need for regular aid and attendance - and mailing it to the PMC for the veteran's state of residence. You can have a doctor fill out the examination information section. You can also submit additional documents to support your claim:

1. Details about what you usually do during the day and how you get to places.
2. Details that help support or show what kind of illness, injury, or mental or physical disability affects your ability to do things such as taking a bath

3. Other evidence, such as a doctor's report, that shows you need aid and attendance or housebound care

If the veteran is in a nursing home, he/she must also fill out a request for nursing home information in connection with the claim for aid and attendance by completing VA form 21-0779. The veteran can apply in person at their local VA regional office near his/her home of residence or by calling the VA at 1-800-827-1000 to get the correct mailing address based on current residence.

There are two types of pension applications. The first type of pension is for veteran households with low income and few assets. For veterans who are currently living and under the age of 65, medical evidence must also be submitted for proof of total disability. Anyone on social security disability is considered totally disabled for purposes of pension. For living veterans age 65 and older, there is no requirement to be disabled. Single surviving spouses of veterans also have no requirement for disability. These low-income applications may or may not have a need for an additional rating to receive an aid and attendance or housebound allowance.

The second type of pension application is for when the housebound veteran typically has income above the income limit. The applicants may also have significant assets. Some legitimate planning has to occur to make sure that the net worth limit is met. These types of claims almost always involve the high cost of long-term care. These care costs may be for the following types of services:

- Paying for the cost of a nursing home
- Paying for the cost of independent living
- Paying for the cost of assisted living
- Paying for cost of daycare
- Paying members of the family to provide care at home
- Paying professional providers to provide care at home

Keep in mind that these second types of claims require medical evidence for a rating for aid and attendance or housebound benefits. These ratings are required by law for certain medical expenses associated with long-term care. Claims for the second type of pension must be completed on the following forms:

- VA form 21-527EZ – veterans application for pension (for living veteran)
- VA form 21-534EZ – application for dependency and indemnity compensation, death pension, and accrued benefits by a surviving spouse or child
- SF 180 – request pertaining to military records (used to get discharge records)
- VA form 21-0779 – request for nursing home information in connection with claim for aid and attendance
- VA form 21-2680 – examination for housebound status or permanent need for regular aid and attendance (completed by claimant's doctor)
- Care provider certification of services – care provider report (completed by claimant's care provider and used to provide evidence of recurring medical expenses)

Veterans and loved ones who qualify for pension must complete the forms that apply through the eBenefits website or in person at the local VA regional office or by mailing to the address below:

Department of Veterans' Affairs
Pension Intake Center
P.O. Box 5365
Janesville, Wisconsin 53547

Caregiver program

The VA has requested 1.2 billion dollars under the mission act for the caregiver program to start up within two years from Fall of 2019. There has been a delay due to the VA updating the old system of paper documents to the new electronic system.

The VA provides a monthly stipend to relatives or friends who care for eligible veterans that have serious injuries they suffered in the line of duty. The program also offers training, access to health insurance, counseling, and respite care. Caregivers receive yearly checks between $7,800 and $30,000 according to the congressional budget office. The caregiver program provides legal and financial planning services for both the injured veteran and their caregiver.

In order to be eligible for the program, the veteran must need care on a regular basis for at least six months as a result of their service-related injuries that are either physical (including traumatic brain injury) or psychological. You must get a clinical evaluation to determine how much care per week you are eligible to receive. The maximum stipend is for 40 hours per week.

A caregiver must be at least 18 years old and at least one of the following must exist:

1. Someone who lives full-time with the veteran, or willing to do so if designated as the caregiver, or
2. A spouse, son, daughter, parent, stepfamily member, or extended family member of the veteran. You can apply for the caregiver program at the local VA Medical Center or by:
    A. Calling the caregiver support line at 1-855-260-3274.
    B. Veteran and caregiver must apply together by completing VA form 10-10CG-5 - Application for the program of comprehensive assistance for family caregivers. Both the

caregiver and veteran must sign and date the form. Mail the form and supporting documents to:

Program of Comprehensive Assistance for Family Caregivers
Health Eligibility Center
2957 Clairmont Road NE, Suite 200
Atlanta, Georgia 30329-1647

C. Apply in person by bringing the application to your local VA medical center's caregiver support coordinator. Locate the closest caregiver support coordinators at www.caregiver. va.gov.

Proposal to reduce rating/rating reduction

The VA routinely conducts compensation and pension examinations (C&P) or QTC exams every two or three years after the veteran has been awarded a disability to determine if his/her condition has improved or has gotten worse. In addition, the VA will mail letters to the address on file proposing to reduce the veteran's disability, especially the higher your rating gets, because they know you will soon be eligible for 100% P&T.

You have 60 days to respond to the proposal letter to reduce your disability rating to the regional office. If you do not challenge or respond, reduction becomes final on the 60th day. Once the VA has made a decision to reduce your rating, they will mail you a letter stating your rating has reduced. At this point, you have one year to file an appeal on VA form 10182, which I will discuss later.

Always respond to VA letters, especially proposals to reduce your rating, otherwise you're making the VA rater's job easy simply by not putting up a fight. It is very important to **keep your address and phone number updated with the VA**. I recommend you go back to your doctor to get an updated independent medical opinion stating your condition(s) have gotten worse since your last evaluation. Include symptoms from the rating chart for the higher disability you're seeking and return the documents certified from the post office. By doing so, if you have to appeal later on, you will have proof of the date you mailed off the documents and who at the VA signed for your response letter.

Always read the back of the VA correspondent letters for deadlines and where to send documents. The VA ultimately does not want to assign veterans 100% P&T and does not want to pay veterans $3,000 a month. I saw this first hand as a former employee at the Veterans' Benefits Administration. The VA would rather deny veterans because the regional offices get bonuses at the end of each year for every veteran they have denied or reduced. This is a shame and disgrace before God, to make it difficult for veterans to get the benefits they deserve.

Since a rating reduction or a proposal to reduce a rating is not a denial, you cannot hire a lawyer at this stage. It is important to respond to the VA with an independent medical opinion (IMO) letter from your doctor proving your disability has gotten worse to prevent the VA from reducing your disability rating. It will be a setback for you if you do not challenge or respond to the VA's proposal letter to reduce your rating. Then you will have to start the process all over again and you will lose all momentum in reaching 100% P&T.

Situations in which the VA can reduce a veteran's rating

1. The VA finds improvement in veteran's disability that is stabilized or has been at the same level for 5 years or more.
2. The VA finds there is an improvement in a disability for an unprotected rating, or one that is less than 100% and has been in effect for less than 5 years.
3. The veteran has been in jail or prison for more than 60 days.
4. The veteran has total disability individual unemployability (TDIU) and decides to go to work. TDIU is temporary because the veteran's condition can improve or get worse. Veteran must be on TDIU at least five years before the VA assigns veteran permanent and total (P&T) status. Veteran must file a claim for permanent and total (P&T) on VA form 526EZ. Don't wait for the regional office to do it for you. It will never happen!!!

Why veterans are denied benefits

Veterans can hire an attorney to file an appeal after receiving a denied letter in the mail from the VA. In my opinion, veterans are denied benefits because they do not know their rights, or the rules and regulations concerning disabilities that are written by Congress. I received many denied letters from the regional office. I never accepted them. I just became more educated on the laws and I was able to hold the regional office and the judge accountable according to the law! I read and studied the rules and regulations.

Many times when the regional office sends veterans letters of denials, they don't list the reasons but make up any excuse. The regional office sometimes lies to the veteran. Sometimes documents are shredded and destroyed. The regional office purposely and strategically withholds funds that belong to veterans and receive Christmas bonuses at the end of the year for doing so. Trust me, I worked at the Veterans' Benefits Administration and witnessed it for myself. Directors received millions of dollars, which was stolen from the VA bank account that belongs to disabled veterans and their family members who are paid for by taxpayers!

I have listed the main reasons below why veterans are denied, and it is written in law. So read the law that states why veterans are denied to ensure you receive your due compensation. Legally, the reasons why veterans are denied are as follows:

1. No current medical diagnosis of a disability by a doctor
2. No clear "nexus letter" to prove service connection by a doctor
3. No letter of explanation of severity or chronicity of symptoms from doctor
4. No proof of in-service injury that occurred during active duty, illness, or event and condition continues to present day
5. Lack of medical evidence with "ongoing medical treatment" during military service and after military service

6. Veteran did not attend their compensation and pension (C&P) or QTC exam
7. Veteran failed to keep current address updated in computer system
8. Veteran used the wrong forms to apply for disability
9. No evidence of current disability symptoms
10. Missed VA disability form deadlines to respond to letters
11. Not responding to VA letters proposing to reduce their disability, which can force a veteran to become homeless and have to start the process all over! Veteran must go back to the doctor to get updated letters showing he/she is still getting ongoing treatment and conditions have gotten worse.

Purpose of VA routine C&P or QTC exams

As I stated before, veterans are scheduled for routine C&P examinations approximately every two or three years, unless they have been awarded permanent and total status. Congress has written laws concerning rules and regulations on how to perform the routine examinations to ensure fair treatment to all veterans.

Veterans should bring a witness or family member who is familiar with his/her condition because the examiner has been known to lie, which could cause a veteran to lose benefits. You should also wear a watch to record what is being said during the meeting if you file an appeal later on. I recommend you never stop going to the doctor because the purpose of the VA C&P exams is to verify if you are continuing to get ongoing treatment. If you have stopped going to the doctor or stopped taking medications, it is highly likely that the VA will reduce or take away your disability.

In most cases, the VA assumes the veteran's disability will get better over time, especially if he/she is rated 50% or higher. The VA will slowly chip away benefits if the veteran does not have updated letters from their doctors stating disability has gotten worse since the last exam! According to VA rules and regulations governing the regional office's C&P exams, the law states the following:

"Request a review examination whenever:

1. There is a need to verify either the continued existence or the current severity of a disability
2. It is likely that a disability has improved
3. Evidence indicates there has been a material change in a disability
4. The current rating may be incorrect, or
5. It is otherwise required by the regulation or diagnostic code (DC) under which the veteran is service-connected (SC)"

VA rating protections

Veterans have certain protections from the VA reducing or taking away disabilities, which Congress has written in the law. A lot of times, veterans lose their benefits for lack of knowledge. Veterans accept anything coming from the regional office as final even when he/she falls under VA rating protections. The law states the VA cannot schedule future exams to reduce or take away veteran's benefits as follows:

"Do not establish a future examination control in cases when:

1. The disability is static, without material improvement over five years
2. The disability is permanent in character and of such nature that there is no likelihood of improvement
3. The veteran is over 55 years of age (except under unusual circumstances or where required by regulation)
4. The evaluation is 10 percent or less, or
5. The combed evaluation would not change even if the reexamination resulted in a reduced evaluation for one or more disabilities."

5-year rule

A veteran who has had the same rating for five years or longer is "stabilized." The VA must show a continued improvement in your condition, which means that the VA cannot use just one re-examination to show "sustained" improvement. The VA must prove through medical records, in addition to a C&P re-examination, that the veteran's condition has shown substantial improvement.

10-year rule

The VA cannot terminate a veteran's benefits if they have been rated for the same condition for a period of at least 10 years unless there is evidence of fraud. However, the VA can still reduce a veteran's rating under the 10-year rule.

20-year rule

The VA cannot reduce a rating that a veteran has been rated for 20 years straight below the original rating level that was given when he/she first put in the claim.

In addition, VA cannot terminate veterans' benefits after 20 or more years. In other words, by law if a veteran has "ongoing treatment" and documentation submitted to VA regional office for 20 years, the veteran automatically becomes eligible for permanent & total (P&T) status. The veteran will no longer be subject to C&P Exams every 2 years. But veterans must put it in writing on a letter to VA that you are requesting VA to find you permanent & total (P&T). Do not wait for the VA to assign you P&T status because it will never happen when VA is constantly trying to find ways to chip away your rating without your knowledge. You must be proactive with your claims! You should also submit medical evidence that shows your service-connected disability or disabilities are not going to improve in the future. To Improve your chance, request your private doctor to write a nexus letter or independent medical opinion stating your disabilities are not going to improve in the future!

Veteran's disability claims neglect

I have worked at the vet center, the VA hospital, and the Veterans Benefits Administration (VBA). I have witnessed how the VA purposely delays and denies veterans their due benefits. As I am writing this book, the current administration has stripped away disability benefits questionnaire (DBQ) forms in which veterans can describe in detail their condition(s) which will ultimately help him/her win VA claims. Just another case in which the current administration and the VA attempts to take away the total disability individual unemployability (TDIU) from veterans who are 55 years or older.

You must know the regulations concerning TDIU. A veteran does not have permanent status on TDIU. TDIU is subject to C&P exams every three years, and the VA conducts audits with social security to verify the veteran has not worked. If a veteran has worked on a job while on TDIU, the VA will reduce his/her benefit. You must fill out the appropriate form to request that the VA award you TDIU with permanent and total (P&T) status. And then you will not be subject to future exams.

While the COVID-19 has all of our attention, it is used as a distraction for the current administration and the VA, making it difficult for veterans to get their benefits. It's hypocritical to have photo ops and appear on tv honoring veterans on Memorial Day May 2020 while behind the scenes, the administration is taking away their benefits. As a veteran and former employee at the VA, I feel the current administration does not appreciate military members and veterans for the sacrifice they made while in the Armed Forces. I witnessed this as a former employee at the vet center, the Veterans' Benefits Administration, and the VA medical center. I have witnessed the following:

1. Many veterans can't get to medical centers because they live far away and do not have transportation.

2. Many veterans are facing wait times of months, or even years, just to see a doctor for their injuries.
3. The center for investigative reporting analyzed claims and found an error rate of 38%. This is why every veteran must file appeals.
4. The regional office did not have veterans' files to review when determining rating assignments but denied veterans anyway without proper due process.
5. Most C&P examiners did not have the veteran's file to review when conducting a C&P exam!
6. The federal government says that between 50% and 70% of veterans' claims were unjustly denied by the VA. Congress recently approved additional VA funding to solve the problem of denied veterans' claims, but VA regional office directors are still stealing the money as reported a few years ago in VA scandals.
7. 20,000 veterans have died while waiting for their disability claims to be processed. That means 50 veterans die each day without having known whether the country appreciated their sacrifices.
8. The VA ended 2012 with approximately 900,000 pending claims. More than two-thirds of those claims were older than 125 days, the time considered by the VA to be in a "backlog status."
9. Disabled veterans were not considered for TDIU and denied TDIU because they are paid at 100% rate - $3,000 month - and it takes a big chunk of money out of the VA's budget.
10. During the Reagan/Bush administration, more than 40,000 veterans were removed from the TDIU rolls, not because they were working, but because veterans failed to filed appeals and didn't have knowledge of their rights. Within a ten-year period, the VA reduced their budget by $80 million.
11. In an audit of the VA disability compensation system at 16 regional offices, the VA office of the inspector general estimates that the rating staff incorrectly processed 23% of the 45,000 claims inspected.

12. According to data from the office of personnel management, the VA claims processors shared $5.5 million in bonuses in 2011. The VA gave some claims processors bonuses for outstanding performance, which effectively encouraged them to avoid processing claims that needed extra work to document veterans' injuries. Other claims were ignored or set aside by workers so they could keep their jobs, meet performance standards or, in some cases, collect extra pay, said VA claims processors and union representatives. I witnessed this as a former employee at the VBA. And as a veteran myself seeking benefits, it took me 21 years of appealing to the Board of Veterans' Appeals in DC to win my cases and overturn the VA regional office's decision of denying me time after time for no reason!

Clear and unmistakable error claim (CUE)

Veterans can file a claim for clear unmistakable error (CUE) if he/she has proof that the regional office has made an error in deciding their claims. **You can file a CUE claim simply by writing or typing a letter explaining in detail who made an error, what error was made, dates, and what VA laws the regional office violated.**

File a CUE claim when errors were made in reducing or taking away benefits with no justified explanation. An example would be if a veteran was denied for TDIU because he/she did not meet the provisions of 38 code of federal regulation 4.16 (a). If the veteran is unemployable because of mental health issues or psychological disability rated less than 70%, then he/she should **file an appeal if the letter is dated within the last 12 months on VA form 10182** or **file and re-submit a new TDIU application on VA form 526EZ if it has been more than 12 months since being denied.**

When I filed my CUE, I wrote in detail a three-page letter to the judge in DC. The judge ruled in my favor and gave me an increase because the error affected all of my other claims in totality! This was a major game changer in keeping my benefits and eventually getting permanent and total disability.

There's a rating protection law that states if a veteran has had a rating for 20 years, the veteran is eligible for permanent and total status. But the veteran has to write the VA requesting P&T. I wrote the VA twice requesting P&T and eventually was awarded P&T once I filed a CUE claim to the judge in DC. I appealed the regional office four times. I took ownership of my claims, studied VA rules and regulations, and did the leg work by completing all of my doctor's appointments and taking my medications. Veterans can appeal or file a clear unmistakable error claim by writing a statement with supporting evidence. You can use the following statement:

"The VA regional office purposely continues to commit obvious errors of fact and law in efforts to delay and deny my claims."

VA regulation definition of a clear unmistakable error (CUE)

Under 38 CFR 3.105(a) a clear and unmistakable error (CUE) exists if all three of the following requirements are met:

A. Either the correct facts, as they were known at the time, were not before the adjudicator (e.g., the adjudicator overlooked them) or the statutory or regulatory provisions existed at the time were incorrectly applied

B. The error must be the sort which, had it not been made, would have manifestly changed the outcome at the time it was made

C. The determination must be based on the record and the law that existed at the time of the prior adjudication in question

Veterans must always respond to VA letters in order to maintain their benefits or the VA will reduce or take away your ratings. The VA regional office refused to process my claim for total disability individual unemployability (TDIU) that I submitted four years prior to receiving a proposal to reduce my PTSD. The regional office has a game: hoping that veterans forget when they file claims! I waited four years for the regional office to process my claim until I received the proposal to reduce my PTSD. As a result, I responded by challenging the proposal to reduce my PTSD and filing a CUE claim. I wrote a two-page letter with my appeal to the judge in Washington, DC. The judge ruled in my favor and I won the CUE claim with an increase. And that canceled out the proposal to reduce my PTSD simply because I responded to the letter and challenged the VA regional office. If I did not respond, it would have sent a message to the regional office that it's ok to take away my benefits! The VA knows many veterans are too busy to read the letters or don't understand the importance of responding or challenging the regional office's decision. And as a result of not responding to the regional office letters, it makes their job easy - to just reduce veterans' ratings or write a denied letter. The VA regional office was forced to back pay me for four years because I knew the law and challenged their decision. I wrote the following statements to prove my CUE claim:

- I feel the VA regional office incorrectly decided my claims without collecting and considering all the medical records from my doctors. The VA regional office never mailed my signed release of medical records form to my doctors. My doctors confirmed they never received a form requesting my medical records.
- The VA regional office has demonstrated a pattern of not requesting medical records from my doctors, and when I submit the medical evidence myself, the VA regional office rejects the medical records or loses the documents in order to justify denying me.
- The VA regional office has demonstrated a pattern of not giving me my due process and not requesting my medical records from doctors, resulting in them denying me of due benefits and denying me of a fair decision.
- The VA regional office purposely continues to commit obvious errors of fact and law in efforts to delay, deny, or overturn the board's decision of processing and expediting my claims for PTSD and chronic back pain.
- The VA regional office did not have my c-file at their office when they made their decision. They denied me without having all the medical evidence.
- The C&P examiner did not have my c-file during the exam and when they wrote their opinion on the report.
- The VA raters and C&P examiner did not have proper education or experience in the complexities of medicine nor the VA laws -38 CFR (code of federal regulations) when they denied me in their opinions.

- My conditions have gotten worse, even with ongoing treatment, based on my doctors' nexus letters with new medical evidence from my chiropractor for my chronic back condition and my psychologist for my chronic PTSD. Please consider all these medical evidences in your decisions fairly.

VA patient advocacy

There are benefits of visiting the patient advocacy office at the VA hospital. First, any time a veteran files a complaint against the hospital, it becomes part of their medical records and can be reviewed by a judge later when he/she files an appeal. Second, if a veteran feels they are not treated fairly by a nurse or doctor, he/she can request to be assigned to another team. (This happened to me when I moved to another state and the doctor documented false notes in my VA medical records. I was able to pick this up because I always monitored what the nurses and doctors documented in my file each month when I visited the VA hospital. This was a game changer! That would have prevented me from getting my disability.) It is very important to monitor VA medical notes because you don't want to waste your time with a nurse or doctor who is documenting false information in your medical records that can be used against you. **Patient advocacy records are part of your medical records and can be used in your favor if you file an appeal later on.**

You win when you appeal to the Board of Veterans' Appeals (BVA)

If your claim is denied by the regional office, I recommend all veterans hire an attorney to appeal claims to the judge in Washington, DC due to the fact that as of February 2019, the VA changed the appeals process and it has become more complicated.

There are a few good reasons to appeal a denied claim from the regional office. First, the raters have no experience in dealing with VA laws that are written by Congress in regard to veterans' disabilities. Second, VA raters do not have experience in medicine. Third, the VA raters do not have experience in occupational limitations imposed by injuries or illnesses that veterans struggle with. This is where the VA can continue to make it difficult for veterans because they know veterans likewise do not understand the rules, regulations, and the process.

Also, the VA can continue to give the veteran the "run around." The decision review officer can cheat the veteran of back pay (based on the effective date) if the DRO grants veteran disability. The DRO can agree with the veteran service representative who denied the claim in the first place and deny the veteran again at the regional office. At this point, the veteran has the opportunity to forward the appeal to the judge in DC.

Therefore, to avoid all of the confusion and avoid the VA regional office taking advantage of you, I recommend hiring an attorney once you receive a denial letter. This will help speed up the process. And by law, attorneys cannot charge you upfront fees but rather will receive a small percentage if the lawyer helps the veteran win their appeal. The small fee the lawyer receives from your back pay is well worth it, and you will be set for life once you receive permanent and total status - and no more future C&P exams! I decided to accept 90% TDIU with permanent and total status because I am being paid at 100% rate and I have the same benefits as a veteran with 100% P&T.

Veterans' options when denied a claim from the regional office

If you receive a denied letter from the regional office, there are three options below you can choose from. Due to constant changes in the process, I recommend calling the VA regional office at their hotline 800-827-1000 or the Board of Veterans' Appeals in Washington, DC at 800-923-8387 to verify the correct forms and procedures. **You can pick only one of the following three options.** Please note that **options 1 and 2 are claims only** that must be submitted to the VA Evidence Intake Center to be processed at the regional office. And **option 3 is to file an appeal** to the Board of Veterans' Appeals with a judge in Washington, DC. All three options should be submitted to the Evidence Intake Center in Janesville, Wisconsin. Once the Evidence Intake Center receives claims or appeals, they will distribute applications to the appropriate department. Veterans should keep originals and submit only copies if they are mailing applications.

Option 1: File a **supplemental claim - VA form 20-0995** - and send it to the Evidence Intake Center. You can **submit new and relevant evidence** that the regional office did not have when they reviewed your claim before. Relevant evidence is evidence that could prove or disprove something in your claim.

Please keep in mind that it is quicker to go to each of your doctors and request your medical records instead of waiting for the VA to request your records, which could take up to twelve months. And sometimes the VA will claim they never received your records. So I recommend putting in the leg work to speed up the claim, which is a game changer! You should seek all medical evidence from private doctors, VA hospital records, military records, and federal facility records to submit to the address below:

Department of Veteran Affairs
Claims Intake Center
P.O. box 5235
Janesville, Wisconsin 53547-5235

Fax #: 1-844-531-7818

Or

Option 2: File a **higher-level review claim - VA form 20-0996** - and send to the Evidence Intake Center. A decision review officer at the regional office will take another look at the previously denied decision from the regional office to see if it can be changed based on any errors made by the staff. Please note that **no new evidence can be submitted.** So please make sure you have all the evidence you need and do not expect any more medical evidence from doctors.

A higher-level review claim is when a veteran disagrees with the regional office's decision; you can have a senior reviewer at the regional office take a new look at your case. The decision review officer (DRO) at the regional office will determine whether the decision can be changed based on a difference of opinion or errors. You can request a higher-level review on both initial claims and a supplemental claim. **You have one year from the date stamped on the letter to file a higher-level review claim.** You can complete the higher-level review on the eBenefits website. You can choose to have a different regional officer from a different city or state review your claim. You can fax or mail your higher-level review claim to the address and fax below:

Department of Veteran Affairs
Claims Intake Center
P.O. box 5235
Janesville, Wisconsin 53547-5235
Fax #: 1-844-531-7818

Or

Option 3: File an **appeal decision review request - VA form 10182.** If you received a decision or higher-level decision from the regional office and you disagree and would like one or more issues to be decided by a veterans law judge in Washington, DC, you can file a clear unmistakable error (CUE) against the regional office in a letter format. Make sure you know the laws that the regional office violated in their decision making and quote the laws in a typed letter. It's hard to be granted CUE claims, but it is a game changer! Submit appeals - VA form 10182 and CUE claim - to the following address below:

Board of Veterans' Appeals
Attention: Intake Center
P.O. box 27063
Washington, DC 20038

Fax #: 1-844-678-8979

Veterans have the right to appeal decisions made by the VA regional office to the Board of Appeals in Washington, DC for consideration by a veteran's law judge. The traditional appeal process is the best method to get your appeal to an independent judge who will apply the law in your best interest. Keep in mind that the raters at the VA regional offices are not law judges and must do what their supervisors tell them to do in order to keep their jobs even with all the necessary supporting documents in a veteran's file.

I recommend not waiting until the last minute to submit paperwork. The sooner you respond to VA letters, the faster the VA can process your claim or appeal. The board does not have a duty to assist you in collecting additional evidence, but you can get free help at the regional office on claims and appeals from your chosen veteran service organization, like American Legion, Disabled American Veteran, or an experienced lawyer dealing with veterans' appeals.

There may come a time when the judge reviews the appeals and may remand or send your appeal back to the regional office for additional work. I recommend hiring an accredited VA attorney to fight your appeals in Washington, DC. I will list the benefits of hiring a VA attorney in the next chapter.

The goal of an appeal is to send your denied claim to the Board of Veterans' Appeals in Washington, DC who makes the final decisions on appeals. An attorney or agent may represent you. You have the option to travel to DC with your lawyer to a hearing in Washington, DC or at a VA regional office, or you can attend by videoconference.

You have another option: hiring a lawyer from another state since the VA is a federal agency. The lawyers have a pin number that gives them access to VA computer systems so that they can pull up a veteran's file. The attorney must know your VA file number to access your VA file in order to process your appeals.

You have one year to appeal from the date stamped on the denial letter from the regional office if you expect to receive years of back payment.

In the past, veterans could file an appeal directly to a judge in DC, but the workload has become too much for a few judges. As a result, the VA changed the process by having veterans' appeals be initiated and reviewed by a decision review officer at the regional office where the veteran's claim was denied in the first place. So the VA regional office now has more power over veteran's appeals. Therefore, it is very important to take your denial letter to a VA accredited attorney who will work in your best interest and knows the rules and regulations concerning appealing claims to the Board of Veterans Affairs.

The VA will send a veteran a statement of the case describing what facts, laws, and regulations were used in deciding the case. At this point, the veteran has several options in filing their appeals to the BVA. This is where it gets complicated. The VA changed the rules of the game on February 2019 concerning VA Appeals. I will give you the pathway that I took. I forwarded my appeals to the Board of Veterans' Affairs for a judge to give me fair and just decisions, which has worked four times in my 21 years of fighting the VA regional office. My method may not apply to every veteran. That's why I recommend hiring an attorney to file your appeals. Never settle with decisions made at the regional office because they have many tricks to cheat veterans of their benefits without the veterans even knowing it.

When I received a denial letter or a letter keeping me at the same percentage, I filed a VA form 21-0958 - notice of disagreement. I mailed and faxed it to the Department of Veterans' Affairs Evidence Intake Center. I also sent a copy to the Board of Veterans' Appeals in Washington DC for backup because the regional office will sometimes lose paperwork or even shred paperwork.

Benefits of hiring an attorney to file appeals

It is in your best interest to hire a veteran's attorney to file for TDIU claim and file appeal on denied claims. Keep in mind, your lawyer is as good as you, meaning that you must learn the laws and how to apply them for yourself to make sure your lawyer is working in your best interest. If you have received a denial letter, immediately contact a veteran's attorney with experience working for veterans to file appeals. By law, the attorney will not charge money upfront to fight the VA regional office. But the attorney will be paid between 10%-20% of your back pay once you win the appeal. After receiving permanent and total status, you will be set for life and can relax and enjoy your benefits! Some benefits of hiring a VA accredited attorney include:

1. Knowledge of the changing laws and experience navigating complex issues with the VA.
2. Get correct rating on your benefits you are not aware of.
3. Get correct amount of compensation.
4. Attorneys have access to the VA system for updated status of your claim.
5. Obtaining other benefits veteran may not be aware of.
6. Keep case on track - no deadlines missed.
7. Able to develop medical link between veteran's medical evidence and the rules and regulations VA must follow when they decide your claims.

Because the appeals process, called Appeals Modernization Act, changed on February 19, 2019, has gotten so complex and difficult to understand, veterans have a high chance of losing their appeals, missing out on a higher rating, and missing out on hundreds of thousands of dollars. That is why I recommend seeking assistance from a VA accredited attorney to file all appeals on your behalf. A lawyer has experience fighting the VA. A lawyer will meet deadlines for filing paperwork and prevent you from losing out on thousands of dollars of back pay. A lawyer will also ensure you receive the correct rating and could reduce years of fighting the VA in helping you receive permanent and total disability.

The final Board of Veterans' Appeals decision is made at the US Court of Appeals for Veterans Claims, which is an independent body, not a part of the Department of Veterans Affairs. If you are not satisfied with an appeal decision from the Board of Veterans' Affairs, you can take your appeal higher to the US Court of Appeals. The deadline to file is 120 days after the Board of Veterans' Appeals decision. It does not hold trials or receive new evidence!

If you are not satisfied with the BVA's decision on any or all of the issues - denied or dismissed - you have several options:

1. File with the board a motion for revision of BVA decision based on clear and unmistakable error (CUE).
2. File with the board a motion for reconsideration of BVA decision.
3. File with the board a motion vacate BVA decision or cancel pending appeals.
4. Appeal to the United States Court of Appeals for veterans' claims (higher court); 120 days to file.

Please be aware that there is no time for filing a motion for reconsideration, a motion to vacate, or a motion for revision based on clear and unmistakable error with the board, or a claim to reopen at the VA regional office.

If you decide to start an appeal to a higher court, you have 120 days from the date of decision on the letter received. You can file a notice of appeal with the court. For more information about the notice of appeals, the procedure for filing, the motion to waive the filing fee if experiencing hardship, and anything concerning the court's rules, visit the court's website at: http://www.uscourts.cavc.gov. Download the forms and fax them to (202) 501-5848. You can file or appeal directly to the United States Court of Appeals for Veterans' Claims:

Clerk, US Court of Appeals for Veterans' Claims
625 Indiana Avenue, NW, Suite 900
Washington, DC 20004-2950

Four different 100% SC disability classifications in the VA system:

1. **100% schedular rating** - a veteran's disabilities total 100% but he/she is able to work. The veteran is still subject to future C&P examinations and their **rating is not protected.** This can result in rating reductions unless he/she becomes permanent and total.

2. **100% total disability individual unemployability (TDIU)** - a veteran is not able to work. The veteran is still subject to future C&P examinations and their **rating is not protected unless he/she is awarded permanent and total after five years being on TDIU.** The VA conducts audits every year to verify if a veteran has been working. If a veteran is found to be working with TDIU status, the VA will reduce his/her rating down to around 10% and take away TDIU status, which pays at least $3,000 month! This may cause the veteran to become homeless and have to start the process all over again!

   Veterans are eligible to apply for total disability individual unemployability if he/she has one disability rated at 60%, such as PTSD by itself, or a combination of disabilities with 70% combined rating with one of those disabilities rated at 40% or greater. Please be aware that the VA will play tricks like not processing a TDIU claim or just denying a TDIU claim due to lack of evidence linking your military service to your inability to work. I recommend hiring an accredited veteran's attorney to file for individual unemployability to avoid all the traps, pitfalls, and landmines of the VA.

The veteran must submit the following forms. The first is **VA form 21-4192 - a request for employment information in connection with claim for disability benefits - to be completed by current and former employers.** The second form is **VA form 21-8940 - application for increased compensation based on unemployability - to be completed by the veteran.** This was a big game changer for me when I received 70% PTSD! Veteran can also qualify with 70% general depression. You only need 60% for one disability to qualify for TDIU!!!

3. **100% permanent and total (P&T)** - a veteran can still work if he/she is classified with a 100% schedular rating. No future C&P exams will be scheduled. After 20 years of ongoing treatment, the veteran's rating is protected from being reduced! You can request the VA to grant P&T status if you are eligible. It must be done in writing on VA **form 21-526 EZ – application for disability compensation and related compensation benefits.** Don't wait for the VA to grant you P&T status because it may never happen. You must have been on TDIU for approximately five years straight, cannot find or keep employment due to service-connected conditions, and then VA will award you with permanent & total status.

4. **100% temporary** due to SC surgery and hospitalization. This rating can remain in effect for 1-13 months. The rating can then be reduced! The veteran must complete VA **form-21-526EZ - application for disability compensation and related compensation benefits.**

Post-traumatic stress disorder (PTSD) rating scale

100% Total occupational & Social Impairment

Total occupational and social impairment, due to such symptoms as: gross impairment in thought processes or communication; persistent delusions or hallucinations; grossly inappropriate behavior; persistent danger of hurting self or others; intermittent inability to perform activities of daily living (including maintenance of minimal personal hygiene); disorientation to time or place; memory loss for names of close relatives, own occupation, or own name.

70% Occupational and Social Impairment, with deficiencies

Occupational and social impairment, with deficiencies in most areas, such as work, school, family relations, judgment, thinking, or mood, due to such symptoms as: suicidal ideation; obsessional rituals which interfere with routine activities; speech intermittently illogical obscure, or irrelevant; near-continuous panic or depression affecting the ability to function independently, appropriately and effectively; impaired impulse control (such as unprovoked irritability with periods of violence); spatial disorientation; neglect of personal appearance and hygiene; difficulty in adapting to stressful circumstances (including work or a worklike setting); inability to establish and maintain effective relationships.

50% Occupational and Social Impairment with reduced reliability

Occupational and social impairment with reduced reliability and productivity due to such symptoms as: flattened affect; circumstantial, circumlocutory, or stereotyped speech; panic attacks more than once a week; difficulty in understanding complex commands; impairment of short- and long-term memory (e.g., retention of only highly learned material, forgetting to complete tasks); impaired judgment; impaired abstract thinking; disturbances of motivation and mood; difficulty in establishing and maintaining effective work and social relationships.

30% Occupational and Social Impairment with occasional decrease

Occupational and social impairment with occasional decrease in work efficiency and intermittent periods of inability to perform occupational tasks (although generally functioning satisfactorily, with routine behavior, self-care, and conversation normal), due to such symptoms as: depressed mood, anxiety, suspiciousness, panic attacks (weekly or less often, chronic sleep impairment, mild memory loss (such as forgetting names, directions, recent events).

10% Occupational and Social Impairment due to mild or transient symptoms

Occupational and social impairment due to mild or transient symptoms which decrease work efficiency and ability to perform occupational tasks only during periods of significant stress; or symptoms controlled by continuous medication.

0% A Mental Condition has been formally diagnosed

A mental condition has been formally diagnosed, but symptoms are not severe enough either to interfere with occupational and social functioning or to require continuous medication.

Mental health

Veterans who served overseas in a combat operation may be eligible for mental counseling at no cost at the Veteran's Resource Center. For more information on this, visit https://www.myhealth.va.gov/mhv-portal-web/.

I experienced a lot while deployed to Iraq in February 2003. Those experiences forever changed my life. I had nightmares and flashbacks. I enrolled in PTSD group counseling and PTSD individual counseling at the VA medical center. Later, I transferred to private doctors for PTSD treatment because, being employed at the VA hospital in the mental health department as a check-in clerk, I discovered in a staff meeting that my name and social security number, along with other veterans, were listed to co-workers. At that moment, I realized that my HIPPA rights were violated. I was an employee and veteran at the same time, getting mental health treatment from doctors who were also my co-workers. My name and social security number should never have been on the list of veterans who were getting treatment for PTSD. I had no privacy and my business was exposed to co-workers.

During my active duty service, I was routinely exposed to artillery gunfire while deployed in Iraq (Operation Enduring Freedom). After returning from Iraq, I began to experience intense anxiety, including intrusive recollections of the traumatic events (death of fellow soldiers, artillery gunfire) in the form of distressing dreams, flashbacks, sadness, survivor's guilt, agitation, irritability, concentration problems, detachment, isolation, and withdrawal. As a result, I lost interest in recreational activities. I had intense periods of anger that were difficult to control. I became introverted and withdrew from interactions, preferring to keep people at a distance due to concerns about being assaulted by strangers.

My job while over in Iraq included providing security, preventing terrorists from invading and killing our troops. I was under constant mortar fire in Iraq. I had to survive 120-degree days and 80-degree nights. I also had to transport the enemies in military convoy and drive over IED bombs, which caused me to have constant fear of roadside bombs and that the enemy may have explosives on them.

I have continued panic attacks, waking up at night with cold sweats. Chronic PTSD continues to impact my sleep apnea every night. I sometimes jump up out of bed at night, seeing my head chopped off, dripping blood, while the ISIS fighters hold up their sword over my bed. I jump up and grab my crowbar under the mattress and check all doors and windows to make sure they're locked and no one broke into my house. I also check the perimeter of my house for an extra sense of security.

It is very difficult to fall asleep with my sleep machine, and even more difficult to get a full night's rest, so I applied for sleep apnea disability. I had to appeal the regional office's decision to the judge in Washington, DC. I was awarded 50% for sleep apnea because I use a c-pap machine.

Please note that it is harder now to be awarded sleep apnea as a primary condition. The way around this is to apply for sleep apnea as a secondary condition to hypertension. In other words, your already service-connected hypertension caused another condition known as sleep apnea. The rule states that you must already have a service-connected disability for hypertension before applying for sleep apnea as a secondary condition to hypertension. Most veterans who have been deployed usually have both hypertension and sleep apnea, which causes him/her to snore loudly when sleeping and eventually need a c-pap machine to help with breathing while sleeping.

I wrote in my stressor letter how sleep apnea, physical pain, and PTSD has affected my daily life during and after work, and how my disabilities have interfered with my ability to get a job and maintain employment. I would fall asleep while driving long distances. I would feel fatigued in the middle of the day after eating lunch. I couldn't concentrate on the job due to flashbacks from being in the war. My stressor letter was a game changer! Also, taking medication to help me sleep such as Trazodone and high blood medication to reduce the heart from working too much was another game changer.

I received 70% for PTSD because I was admitted into a private patient mental health care facility and I was deployed in a combat zone in the Iraq war. Whether or not you were admitted into a mental health facility or psychiatric hospital for PTSD carries a lot of weight when the regional office assigns your rating for PTSD.

I was forced to take heavy doses of medication while at the mental health facility. I remember going to the bathroom and falling on the floor, head almost flushed down the toilet. I was holding on to the toilet as if someone was standing over me pushing my head down. The medication was overwhelming I must say.

This series of events affected my job. I had difficulty staying awake at work and concentrating because I could not get a peaceful night of rest due to hypervigilance, startled reactions, and sudden noises from neighbors slamming car doors or hearing helicopters in the area. When I heard a sudden noise, I would jump up out of my chair. And I still do when I hear firecrackers during holidays like Memorial Day, New Year's, and Fourth of July.

I included the PTSD rating scale diagram in my book because PTSD is a "high-value claim," which means it carries more weight compared to small-value claims. This was another game changer for me! Veterans who have been deployed to a combat zone usually get awarded PTSD.

Once a veteran has first been awarded for a disability, the VA will request a C&P exam two or three years later to verify if he/she is continuing to be treated by a doctor. So in order to get and maintain benefits, you must go back to your doctor and request an updated nexus letter stating your conditions have gotten worse. **The nexus letter for PTSD must be written by a mental health doctor** and must match the rating scale with the symptoms you are experiencing. Also, your medical records must match the nexus letter with documentation and notes from when you visited the doctor's office. This is how the rating specialist determines what percentage to award you, which comes directly from the VA rules and regulations manual book written by Congress to ensure every veteran is treated fairly in decision making.

Unfortunately, many veterans are not aware of the VA regulations and give up too easily. But if you study the rules and regulations, you can win the game by holding the VA's feet to the fire. I applied for PTSD because I served in the Iraq war and received several combat awards, which are coded on my DD-214. When the VA verified I served in Iraq, by law it made it easier to establish service connection for PTSD based on the VA rules and regulations written by Congress.

From my experience, a PTSD claim is the quickest route to getting permanent and total, but the VA regional office kept delaying and denying my claims hoping that I would give up. But I kept appealing to the Board of Veterans' Affairs in Washington DC every time they denied me and I never lost a case! It's a shame I had to fight the VA regional office tooth and nail for 21 years. Eventually, the VA regional office was forced by the appeals judge to award me permanent and total because I was eligible **under the 20-year rule that states if a veteran has had a rating for any condition for 20 years, the VA cannot reduce or take away his/her disability.**

I have received several awards coded on my DD-214, including Air Force Achievement Medal, AF Outstanding Unit Award with Valor Device, Air Reserve Forces Meritorious Service Medal with 1 Oak Leaf Cluster, National Defense Service Medal, Global War on Terrorism Expeditionary Medal, Global War on Terrorism Service Medal, Air Force Expeditionary Service Ribbon with Gold Border, AF Longevity Service with 1 Oak Leaf Cluster, Faithful Service Medal, Armed Forces Reserves Medal with "M" Device, and Air Force Outstanding Unit Award with Valor Device. Due to my service and sacrifice, and never giving up fighting the VA, I was finally awarded P&T and all the benefits, rights, and privileges that I was promised.

Many times, the VA raters are not experienced in processing veterans' claims and are not aware of the VA court's status and regulations that govern the application process. To help the VA raters, who may be new on the job, the veteran's psychologist can review the veteran's DD-214 that lists the veteran's combat awards, if any. The psychologist can include the following statement in their nexus letter: (I used the combat awards on my DD-214 as an example.)

"I have reviewed the veteran's DD-214 medals and awards, which confirms evidence that the veteran engaged in combat operation against an armed enemy and his stressors are related to combat in Iraq where the stressful events occurred. After reviewing VA court's statuettes, regulations, and provisions, the veteran's PTSD claim is a well-grounded claim. The veteran's decorations include Armed Forces Reserves Medal with "M" device and Air Force Outstanding Unit Award with valor device."

Well-grounded claim law

1. Well-grounded claim: VA manual m21-1, chapter 5, paragraph 5.14 (b) (1)

Service connection for PTSD requires medical evidence diagnosing the condition in accordance with 38 CFR 4.125 (a); a link, established by medical evidence between current symptoms and an in-service stressor; and credible evidence that the claimed in-service stressor occurred 38 CFR 3 304 (f).

Conclusive evidence is any evidence the veteran has showing that the area he/she served in was a stressful event. Any evidence supporting the description of the event should be accepted by the VA as part of the veteran's record. If the veteran does not have medical records, but has stressor letters related to combat, the VA rater must accept it along with any decorations coded on his/her DD-214. However, this does not prevent VA raters from making it difficult for combat veterans by requesting additional information before making a decision on the veteran's case. If this occurs, **this is clearly grounds to file a clear unmistakable error (CUE) claim against the VA because it demonstrates the rater was not knowledgeable about the rules and regulations governing PTSD claims when processing the combat veteran's claim for PTSD. Always remember: clear unmistakable error (CUE) is not an appeal but a claim a veteran decides to file.**

The law states no further evidence is required when a veteran has been awarded one of the following awards and should qualify the claim as a well-grounded claim in which the VA must expedite the combat PTSD claim with no further delays.

Evidence that the veteran engaged in combat includes any one of the following awards on his/her DD-214:

- Armed Forces Medal With "M" Device
- Air Force Outstanding Unit Award With Valor Device

- Air Force Cross
- Army Commendation Medal With "V" Device
- Bronze Star Medal With "V" Device
- Combat Action Ribbon
- Combat Infantry Badge
- Combat Medical Badge
- Distinguished Flying Cross
- Distinguished Service Cross
- Joint Service Commendation Medal With "V" Device
- Medal Of Honor
- Navy Commendation Medal With "V" Device
- Navy Cross
- Purple Heart
- Silver Star

2. US Court Of Appeals For Veterans' Claims:
   Zarycki v. Brown and West v. Brown - these cases made it clear that if the claimant engaged in combat with the enemy and alleged stressors are related to such combat, no further evidentiary development will be required by the VA.

How to apply for post-traumatic stress disorder (PTSD)

Veterans who plan to apply for post-traumatic stress disorder (PTSD) with the VA must complete two different forms. The first form is VA **form 21-526EZ - application for disability compensation and related compensation benefits.** The second form that must be completed is VA **form 21-0781 - statement in support of claim for service connection for post-traumatic stress disorder (PTSD).**

Veterans can apply for PTSD disability benefits in one of the following ways:

1. https://va.gov
2. https://eBenefits.gov
3. Mail completed VA form to:
   Department Of Veterans' Affairs
   Claims Intake Center
   P.O. box 4444
   Janesville, Wisconsin 53547-4444
   or
   Fax #: 1-844-531-7818

Veterans and military crisis line

If you or a loved one need immediate help, contact one of the crisis hotlines listed below. Services are free to all service members including members of the National Guard and Reserve, even if you are not registered with the VA or enrolled in VA health care. Many men and women in the military call the crisis hotline every day to get back on track. This is a 24 hour, toll-free suicide prevention service available to anyone in suicidal crisis. You will be routed to the nearest crisis center. Your call is free and confidential.

Veterans crisis hotline - 800-273-8255 (press 1)

National suicide prevention hotline – 800-273-8255

Special monthly compensation

Special monthly compensation is an additional tax-free benefit paid to veterans, their spouses, surviving spouses, and parents. The VA will pay veterans **above the 100% disability rate** for special circumstances if they qualify. There are different categories of special monthly compensation:

Specific severe disabilities: examples include amputation or loss of use, loss of eyesight or bilateral deafness

Aid and attendance: or a severe disability that requires regular supervision or assistance from someone but not a medical professional. Examples include the inability to dress themselves, take care of basic hygiene or feed themselves.

Housebound status: when a veteran is substantially confined to their home because of their service-connected disability and it is reasonably certain that this disability will continue throughout the rest of his/her life.

Tip: A veteran can receive both compensation aid and attendance and individual unemployability benefits at the same time. You can apply for both benefits at the same time also. Individual unemployability benefits are for veterans that cannot work due to their service-connected disabilities. Veterans can complete VA **form 21-526EZ using one of the** following methods:

1. https://va.gov
2. https://eBenefits.gov
3. Mail completed VA form to:
   Department Of Veterans Affairs
   Claims Intake Center
   P.O. box 4444
   Janesville, Wisconsin 53547-4444
   Fax: 1-844-531-7818

3. An accredited representative or agent
4. Veteran can bring their application to nearest VA regional office. Get a stamped copy for your records. If approved, VA will pay starting from the stamped date on the disability form application.

Obstructive sleep apnea

Sleep apnea is a serious sleep disorder that has the potential to kill people if not treated. Sleep apnea affects over 20 million people. Three out of four veterans are denied sleep apnea at the appeals level. You have a better chance of claiming sleep apnea as a secondary condition. (I have listed how in an earlier chapter.) This happens when a person's sleep is interrupted throughout the night and causes a different disability.

Some symptoms of sleep apnea include: waking up through the night, gasping for air; feeling tired the next morning; acid reflux; loud snoring that wakes up spouse, family members, or fellow soldiers; difficulty concentrating; poor memory and confusion because you could not get a restful night of sleep; falling asleep while driving; lack of blood flow in the body; and waking up in the morning with dry mouth and headaches. As a result of the above symptoms, sleep apnea may affect a person's ability to work and keep a job. Sleep apnea disability is meant to replace lost earnings as a result of a military illness. There are three different types of sleep apnea:

- Obstructive sleep apnea - the most common sleep apnea in which the tongue blocks airflow in and out of the throat while sleeping
- Central sleep apnea - this occurs when the brain doesn't send proper signals to the muscles that control breathing.
- Complex sleep apnea - this occurs when a person has both obstructive and central sleep apnea.

In order to receive a sleep apnea disability, a veteran must take a sleep study test with a c-pap machine, preferably with a private doctor who works in his/her best interest. But the VA will automatically schedule veteran to a C&P exam or QTC to see if he/she has sleep apnea.

From my experience working at the VA, I knew the VA typically gives veterans a very difficult time in getting disability for sleep apnea.

That's why I went to a private doctor for the sleep study test. I invested in a $400 c-pap machine back in 2003 immediately after returning home from Iraq. There's a VA law that states a veteran likely has the condition they're seeking if he/she sees a doctor while still on active duty orders. So I recommend seeking treatment to get a sleep study within one year of discharge from active duty so that your diagnosis and treatment will be documented in your military records. If you are in the Reserve or National Guard, I recommend getting a sleep study when you are still on active duty, that way sleep apnea will be documented in your reserve unit's military record.

Make sure you get a copy of your military records before discharge. In fact, make sure you get a physical exam and see a doctor for anything that's hurting you. (Soldiers sometimes think they will always be young, but believe me, one day your body will get old and you will have pain in places you never would have thought.) In essence, you're preparing your medical records for a potential disability(s) later with the VA.

There are two reasons that the VA would deny sleep apnea. The first is that the veteran was not diagnosed as suffering from sleep apnea during military service because it was not documented. Second, the sleep apnea was caused by obesity, and since soldiers are in shape and fit, it's impossible to have suffered from sleep apnea while in the military, and therefore sleep apnea was likely caused by weight gain. The reason for denial will be in the VA letter if they deny you for sleep apnea. The best way to defeat this denial is to get your sleep apnea study done while in the military and submit the sleep study report to your unit so the report will be in your medical records. Also you will take the sleep study while you're in top shape! This is a game changer in beating the VA regional office at its own game!

Like I said, take the sleep study test with a private doctor within the first year after returning from deployment or 6 to 8 months before discharge or retirement. **If anything is hurting or bothering you, get everything documented in your military medical records before leaving the service.** This is a game changer because Congress wrote the law knowing veterans do not have access to doctors during deployment or in a war zone situation. Provisions were made so that veterans can get disabilities easier, especially if he/she seeks treatment within the first year of returning from deployment.

I put this to the test when I returned from Iraq in July 2003. I was still on active duty and had 6 to 8 months to discharge from the Air National Guard. I went on sick call on drill weekend and had it documented in my military records that I was using a c-pap machine for sleep apnea. Once my commander found out about it, by law the military had to send me on 3 months leave without pay from the reserve unit because military personnel cannot be in a combat zone with a c-pap machine - it makes noise and will alert the enemy.

At that time, I was 20% service-connected from the VA for back pain while serving in the reserve. When the VA found out I was on medical leave for 3 months, they deducted 3 months of compensation pay. Before leaving the Air National Guard, I requested a couple of friends to write a lay statement because they witnessed my loud snoring. They also wrote a lay statement for my PTSD and how it changed my whole life after returning from Iraq combat zone. This proved I had an in-service event, injury, disease, or illness that occurred while in the military. It was well documented in my military active duty records while on orders from deployment that I had sleep apnea.

Now I had all the documents that were required by law to receive a disability for sleep apnea, but the regional office still ignored the evidence and denied me anyway. I then had to file an appeal to a judge in DC. The judge back paid me for five years and reimbursed me for the 3 months that the regional office took away my 20% disability pay! And in the meantime, I continued to make my sleep apnea appointments with the VA hospital and my private doctor every 6 months or once a year to verify I was still using the c-pap machine. **Your doctor must prescribe you a c-pap machine and you must sleep with the c-pap machine if you expect to get compensated at 50% rating or higher.**

It is really sad that I had to get a private doctor for every disability I applied for to counter the VA hospital's sleep apnea doctor and VA C&P exams, simply because the VA did not want to compensate me, even though I had all medical documents required under the law. When I first applied for disability, I knew I was going to be in it for the long haul. Faith carried me through for 21 years and it paid off in the end.

Iraq and Afghanistan war veterans have a higher chance of getting sleep apnea. Other injuries include traumatic brain injury, military sexual trauma, and post-traumatic stress disorder. In order to be service-connected for sleep apnea, you must prove that it was aggravated by military service or it occurred while you were in the military. To qualify for sleep apnea disability, you must submit the following documents, including your sleep apnea report and an independent medical opinion from your doctor:

- A sleep study (preferably from a private sleep specialist while on active duty - submit to unit before discharge) of the veteran sleeping with a c-pap machine. I know a few people who took the sleep study with the VA, but the VA gave them the "run around" to avoid having to compensate them. So I did my sleep study with a private doctor using my private insurance with Blue Cross Blue Shield. Submit your sleep study report to the VA.
- A current diagnosis of specific sleep apnea: (OSA, CSA, or COMPSA) confirmed and verified by a sleep study with a c-pap machine.
- An in-service (active duty or while on active duty order from Reserves or National Guard) or sleep apnea as a secondary condition that occurred after military service; event or injury caused veteran's sleep apnea.
- Nexus letter from private sleep specialist (doctor) linking sleep apnea to in-service event or illness. I have provided an example of a nexus letter in an earlier chapter of this book. The doctor must write in the nexus letter that the veteran's military service was "at least as likely as not" the cause of his/her sleep apnea.
- Lay statement from spouse, relative, or fellow comrade from the military unit who can write a letter stating they have witnessed the veteran's symptoms and limitations while on active duty

or deployment and after deployment, noticed a big change in his/her health condition. When writing a lay statement, give specific times, durations, frequency, severity, and a description of symptoms you observed about the veteran.

- Medical evidence showing past and current treatment for sleep apnea; medical records from sleep specialist (proving ongoing treatment).

It is easier for veterans to file sleep apnea as secondary to an already service-connected disability that he/she has been compensated for. In other words, a veteran's service-connected disability caused another disability. If you are already service-connected for PTSD, you can later on file sleep apnea as secondary. Basically, the PTSD service-connected disability caused sleep apnea to occur later after service!

In the case of secondary conditions, you must get a medical nexus opinion letter from a doctor linking the secondary condition to the already service-connected disability.

Sleep apnea is a high-value claim to pursue because you can get up to 100% P&T. Keep in mind, VA doctors usually will not write medical nexus opinions, which you need for disability. So therefore, you will have to be treated for the same conditions by private doctors who will be glad to write medical nexus opinions. This is all part of the VA game that makes it difficult for veterans to get their disability!

VA rating for sleep apnea

Sleep apnea is rated under 38 CFR § 4.97, diagnostic code 6847 – sleep apnea syndromes (obstructive, central, mixed). Veterans are assigned a 0, 30, 50, or 100 percent rating depending on the severity of their condition. There are certain symptoms of sleep apnea – excessive daytime sleepiness, difficulty concentrating, fatigue – that may impact a veteran's ability to work or secure employment.

If you cannot work due to sleep apnea, please also apply for individual unemployability on VA form 526EZ and submit to the VA Evidence Intake Center along with a letter from a doctor stating you can no longer work due to a service-connected disability(s). The VA rating criteria is as follows:

- **100%** - chronic respiratory failure with carbon dioxide retention, the need for a tracheotomy, or *cor pulmonale*. Cor pulmonale is the enlargement or failure of the right side of the heart due to lung disease.
- **50%** – the veteran requires the use of a breathing-assistance device, such as a c-pap machine
- **30%** – the veteran is experiencing persistent daytime hypersomnolence (a condition characterized by chronic daytime sleepiness that does not improve even with sufficient sleep)
- **0%** – the veteran's condition is asymptomatic (i.e. condition that is not producing symptoms) but has a documented sleep disorder

Tip: if a veteran dies from sleep apnea or any service-connected disability, the surviving family members and dependents are eligible and should file a claim for survivor's benefits from the VA.

Migraine headaches

A migraine is a chronic headache. Symptoms of migraines include vomiting, nausea, intense throbbing or pulsing on one side of the head, and being sensitive to light and sound. Migraine attacks can last for hours or days. The pain can be so severe that it interferes with a person's daily activities. You should see a doctor or go to the emergency room immediately if you're experiencing headache with fever, stiff neck, mental confusion, seizures, double vision, numbness or trouble speaking.

You can get compensation for migraines in two ways. The first is claiming an in-service injury with medical records proving you have a diagnosis and have received treatment while on active duty. The second way is claiming migraines as a secondary condition (resulting from an already service-connected disability). The VA rating scale for migraines is as follows:

- 50% - very frequent, 2 or 3 times a month, completely prostrating - entirely bedridden for a period of time, unable to sit or stand up, and prolonged attacks productive of severe economic inadaptability (unable to work)
- 30% - characteristic prostrating attacks occurring on an average of once a month over the last several months
- 10% - characteristic prostrating attacks averaging one every two months over the last several months
- 0% - less frequent attacks

Hypertension or high blood pressure

High blood pressure can lead to heart attacks, kidney failure, and heart strokes. Symptoms of hypertension (high blood pressure) include chest pain, severe headaches, vision problems, fatigue, difficulty breathing, blood in urine, irregular heartbeat, and pounding in chest and neck area.

Veterans who developed hypertension (high blood pressure) during or after military service may be eligible for disability compensation. Hypertension is considered a high-value claim because veterans can get up to 60% rating. This can be a game changer, especially when you have 80% or 90% rating, because technically you will need an additional 50% once you have reached 90% to reach 100% schedular rating, according to VA math.

Hypertension is considered a "presumptive service connection disability" if a veteran or service member was treated by a doctor and received a diagnosis within one year of discharge from active duty. The presumptive service connection disability is much easier to qualify for disability if you met the one-year deadline after release from active duty. Otherwise it will be difficult to prove service connection. If one year has passed, the veteran then has to get a medical opinion from a private doctor.

The VA compensates veterans based on their high blood pressure reading device prescribed and issued by their doctor. Your doctor must show records of taking the blood pressure reading three different days, twice a day. Many veterans do not know they can apply for hypertension, including myself until after I reached permanent and total status. This is why I have included in this book several disabilities to consider claiming if you have been diagnosed with and are currently being treated for a disability.

Below is the rating scale for hypertension:

Diastolic pressure predominantly 130 or more	60%
Diastolic pressure predominantly 120 or more	40%
Diastolic pressure predominantly 110 or more, or systolic pressure predominantly 200 or more	20%
Diastolic pressure predominantly 100 or more, or systolic pressure predominantly 160 or more, or minimum evaluation for an individual with a history of diastolic pressure predominantly 100 or more who requires continuous medication for control	10%

Definition of permanent disability (P&T)

The VA can award veterans 70% P&T, 80% P&T, 90% P&T, or 100% P&T. The goal of every veteran should be permanent & total status to avoid having to keep going back for QTC or C&P exams to prove your disability has gotten worse. According to VA rules and regulations, permanent disability means disabling manifestations are reasonably certain to continue throughout the individual's lifetime. The following examples are from the VA regulations that state a veteran is determined to be permanent & totally (P&T) disabled:

- Evidence at the time of evaluation affirmatively shows that the total disability will continue for the remainder of the person's life.
- Evidence at the time of evaluation does not specifically support that the total disability will continue for the remainder of the person's life but does not show that the condition is likely to improve pursuant to 38 CFR 3.327(b)(2). In such cases, a future examination control is inappropriate, so the total disability rating is static; in the absence of re-evaluation, total disability is likely to continue for the remainder of the person's life.
- At or before the time of maturation of a future examination diary pertinent to the continuation of total disability, the future examination control is canceled.

There are ways to determine if a veteran is permanent & total. You can log on to the eBenefits.gov website to print letters or wait until you receive award letters in the mail. The VA award letter stating permanent and total status should read as follows:

"Dear Mr./Ms. _____, we are providing you with this letter so you may receive **commissary store and exchange privileges** from the Armed Forces. This is to certify that you are an honorably discharged veteran of the Air Force (or other branch you served in) and are entitled to disability compensation (90% individual unemployability) paid at the 100 percent rate due to service-connected disabilities.

This **total disability** is considered **permanent. You are not scheduled for future examinations."**

or

"Dear Mr./Ms. _____, this letter is a summary of the benefits you currently receive from the Department Of Veteran Affairs (VA). We are providing this letter for disabled veterans to use when applying for **benefits such as state or local property or vehicle tax relief, civil service preference, or to obtain housing entitlements and free or reduced state park annual memberships**, or any other program or entitlement in which verification of VA benefits is required.

You are considered to be **totally and permanently disabled,** due solely to your service-connected disabilities.

The effective date of when you became totally and permanently disabled due to your service-connected disabilities: May 13, 2020

We granted basic eligibility to dependents' educational assistance (chapter 35) as of May 13, 2020, the date the review noted your service-connected disabilities were static. Your dependents may be eligible for benefits under **ChampVA."**

Veterans who have permanent and total status are entitled to **free dental** treatment at the VA medical center. Veterans may be **entitled to social security**. For more information, call 800-325-0778 or visit the website: http://www.ssa.gov."

Chapter 35 - Dependents' educational assistance

Disabled veterans' dependents may be eligible for dependents' educational assistance (chapter 35). The VA will pay a monthly allowance for disabled veterans' dependents to attend school full time. The VA will pay a monthly stipend of $1,224 to the veteran's dependents to help pay for tuition and books. Veteran must have achieved permanent and total status, which is written on the veteran's award letter. You must complete VA **form 22-5490 – dependents' application for VA education benefits (under provisions of chapter 33 and 35, of title38, U.S.C).** For more information on this program, visit the website: http://www.gibill.va.gov/benefits/otherprograms/dea.html or call 888-442-4551.

ChampVA dependents healthcare

The Civilian Health and Medical Program of the Department of Veterans Affairs (ChampVA) is a health benefits program in which the Department of Veterans Affairs (VA) shares the cost of certain healthcare and supplies with eligible beneficiaries. To be eligible for the ChampVA program, a dependent must be the spouse or child of a veteran who is permanent and totally disabled from a service-connected disability.

The ChampVA Health Administration, located in Denver, Colorado, can be contacted at 800-733-8387. To apply for ChampVA benefits, you must submit the following documents:

- **VA form 10-10d - application for ChampVA benefits**
- **VA form 10-7959c - other health insurance (OHI) certification**
- Individuals on Medicare, send copy of your Medicare card
- Individuals age 65 or older who are not entitled to Medicare, send copy of social security administration that confirms you're not entitled to Medicare benefits under anyone's social security number
- VA award letter showing veteran is permanently and totally disabled (or death rating for a survivor)
- Veteran's DD-214, certificate of release or discharge from active duty
- Birth certificate/adoption papers for children
- School certification of full-time enrollment for children ages 18-23
- Marriage certificate

Submit your signed ChampVA application to:
VHA Office of Community Care
ChampVA Eligibility
P.O. box 469028
Denver, Colorado 80246-9028
Fax: 1-303-331-7809

Humana care

Humana care is an option for those seeking healthcare treatment from private doctors. You will have to pay monthly premiums. Humana offers Medicare, dental, vision, Medicaid, and pharmacy. If you are receiving Humana and social security, do not pay monthly premiums for both. You should pick which healthcare program is in your best interest. I started paying monthly premiums with Blue Cross Blue Shield from my former employer after I became disabled, and I have Medicare through social security (part a) which is free. So I did not need to sign up for Humana care. But Humana care is a good option for veterans who did not retire from a job. For more information on humana, please visit their website: humana.com

Humana, Inc.

500 W. Main street

Louisville, Kentucky 40202

Medicare through Humana: 800-457-4708

Insurance through employers: 800-448-6262

Medicaid through Humana: 800-477-6931

Humana gold plus integrated (MMAI): 877-912-8880 (TTY: 866-565-8576)

Dental and vision through Humana: 877-877-1051

VA dental treatment

Veterans who are TDIU or have permanent and total status are entitled to free dental treatment at the VA medical center. You must be enrolled at the VA medical center. Contact your primary doctor and request a consult or referral to the dental department. Once the dental office receives consult, they will call you to schedule an appointment.

I attempted to get dental treatment at the VA medical center when I needed a root canal. I was in a lot of pain. Luckily for me, I had insurance to get immediate treatment from a private dentist in my neighborhood. It was on a Saturday morning. I called and I got treatment from my private dentist the same day because I elected to keep Blue Cross when my former employer declared me disabled. That was the best decision I made, even though I have to pay monthly premiums.

Two months passed and I never received a call from the VA dentist. The third month, I called the VA to cancel the request for dental treatment. It pays to have options when it comes to your health. To get immediate treatment from private doctors because you have private health insurance provides peace of mind. There are times that you cannot wait to get treatment at the VA hospital.

Blind rehabilitation services

The VA offers blind rehabilitation services to eligible blind, low vision, or visually impaired veterans to help them regain their independence and quality of life. The veteran's conditions do not have to be related or due to military service. Veterans can contact the nearest Visual Impairment Services Team coordinator (VIST) at the eye clinic in the nearest VA medical center or visit the website: www.va.gov/blindrehab/.

Benefits based on a veteran's seriously disabled child

The VA pays veterans monthly financial compensation if he/she has a "helpless child" in addition to their service-connected disability. A "helpless child" is considered an adult child with a mental/physical disability that causes the child to be incapable of self-sufficiency. Veterans must complete VA form 21-526EZ online - eBenefits website - or submit the form to the Department of Veterans Evidence Intake Center, or take the form to the local VA regional office.

According to the VA, a "helpless child" must meet certain eligibility. They must be:

1. 18 years of age or older
2. The child of a veteran
3. Currently disabled with a permanent incapacity for self-support
4. Diagnosed with a mental/physical disability before the age of 18 that leaves them with a permanent incapacity for self-support

Specially adapted housing/special home adaptation

Veterans and service members with a serious service-connected disability are eligible to get a housing grant from the VA. There are two types of grant programs that exist: the specially adapted housing (SAH) grant and the special housing adaptation (SHA) grant. You may use a grant to buy or build an adapted home or modify an existing home to meet your needs. Veterans must complete VA form 21-526EZ online - eBenefits website - mail form to the Department of Veterans Affairs Evidence Intake Center, or visit the local VA regional office. Call 800-827-1000 for more details.

Some requirements for this program include: loss or loss of use of both legs, loss or loss of use of both arms, blindness, loss or loss of use of one leg, certain severe burn injuries, or certain severe respiratory injuries. These grants can help veterans and service members live independently.

Veterans and service members can use an SAH grant for one of the following:

- Remodel an existing home, if adaptable, to meet your needs.
- Build a specially adapted home on land you already own or land you are buying.
- Apply the grant to the mortgage balance of an adapted home not bought using VA grant funds

Veterans and service members can use an SAH grant for one of the following:

- Adapt a home for you to live in that you or a family member are buying
- Adapt the home you currently live in that you or a family member already own.
- Help you buy a home to live in that's already adapted.

VetSuccess

The VA helps veterans with service-connected disabilities to prepare for, obtain, and maintain suitable employment through the vocational rehabilitation and employment VetSuccess program. First, the VA conducts a comprehensive evaluation to help the veteran determine his/her future career path. Based on your evaluation, VetSuccess provides you with vocational counseling, job-related searches, and other education and training services. VetSuccess is available to recently separated military personnel. In addition, VetSuccess offers assistance to veterans when filing disability claims.

Co-payments

Veterans will not have to pay for medication once they reach 50% or higher at the VA hospital. If you receive care at a VA medical facility, please call the Health Benefits Call Center at 877-222-8387 or notify your local VA medical center of a change in your compensation benefits. The rating may reduce or eliminate your co-payments for VA-provided medical care. You may also be eligible for a refund based on the rating decision. You can contact the VA medication refund at 866-258-2772. Information concerning VA health care eligibility and co-payments is located at: http://www.va.gov/healthbenefits/cost/.

Reimbursement for travel mileage

Veterans rated 30% or higher for disability may be eligible for reimbursement for travel mileage for VA appointments. In some cases, it can be lower than 30%. You must make a request for reimbursement within 30 days of your appointment by completing VA form 10-3542 - veteran/beneficiary claim for reimbursement of travel expenses. You can mail, fax, email, or take the form and receipts in person to the VA medical facility where you were treated. It's best to turn the form in in person. You can contact their office at 877-222-8387.

Clothing allowance

The VA pays veterans $830.56 yearly for clothing that has been damaged by their prosthetic or orthopedic device including a wheelchair or by the medicine they're taking for a skin condition. The money helps veterans purchase new clothes. But the catch is that the veteran must be service-connected or receiving disability payments for their condition in order to qualify for the clothing allowance.

In order to receive a one-time payment for clothing allowance on a yearly basis, you need to **complete VA form 10-8678 - an application for annual clothing allowance.** Once completed, turn the form in at the nearest VA Medical Center's Prosthetics and Sensory Aids Service Office. Or you can call 800-827-1000. If you are approved, you will receive payment between September 1st and October 31st.

Disabled veterans' student loan forgiveness program

Disabled veterans who have been approved for total disability individual unemployability (TDIU) or permanent and total disability are eligible to have their student loans discharged. You should contact your student loan lenders and notify them that you have been deemed unable to work by sending them a doctor's nexus letter, your VA award letter, and your social security award letter. As a result of your disability, the student loan lender will mail a form for you to complete and return along with your social security award letter and VA award letter stating you are being paid at 100% rate due to service-connected conditions. You can also log on to the eBenefits website to print your VA award letter. You can send documents by mail or fax to your student loan lender. Once approved, you will receive a 1099-c - cancellation of debt letter. This was a super game changer for me. It was one of the best feelings - a weight lifted off my shoulders. I would have spent the rest of my life paying off student loans. In fact, under FICO 10, the credit agencies count student loans against you.

Automobile grant

The automobile grant is a tax-free benefit for service-connected veterans or service members to buy a used or new vehicle. The VA pays a one-time payment of no more than $21,488 to help a veteran buy a specially equipped vehicle. You can file a claim for disability compensation and get VA approval before buying a vehicle or adaptive equipment. For the one-time payment, you will need to **complete VA form 21-4502 - application for automobile or other conveyance and adaptive equipment**. Then the VA will pay the dealership directly. The VA also has partnerships with banks to help veterans apply for automobile grants. To be eligible, you must have one of the following service-connected disabilities:

1. Loss or permanent loss of use of one or both feet
2. Loss or permanent loss of use of one or both hands
3. Permanent impairment of vision in both eyes to a certain degree
4. A severe burn injury
5. Amyotrophic lateral sclerosis (ALS)
6. Ankylosis in one or both knees or hips

Disabled veterans' plate

Disabled veterans who are rated permanent and total or total disability individual unemployability can get a free automobile tag from the DMV, which will save veterans thousands of dollars at the dealership and exempt them each year from valorem tax. When you purchase a vehicle at a dealership, submit your VA award letter and the dealership will order a disabled tag electronically to the DMV. The tag will be mailed to your home residence within a few weeks.

Disabled veterans can also apply for a disabled parking permit, which is the blue placard that hangs on the mirror inside the car. You must put in a request for the blue placard tag with your VA primary doctor or private doctor. The handicap parking permit helps veterans with certain conditions that impact their ability to walk short distances. There are six qualifying conditions for a disabled parking permit:

1. Loss of mobility
2. Limited or no use of arms
3. Use of prosthetics
4. Limited vision
5. Cardiac conditions

Property tax and VA funding fees exempted

Disabled veterans who are permanent and total or TDIU are eligible to receive property tax exemption. This benefit varies from state to state. Some states give veterans 100% tax exempts and other states give veterans a discounted rate on property taxes. With total exemptions, veterans are exempted from property taxes between $7,000-$10,000. If you are permanent and total, you can request a waiver of the VA funding fee when purchasing a house. This could save you thousands of dollars.

Free or reduced state park annual membership

Veterans can get free or reduced state park memberships when visiting state and federal parks. You can register for a decal by submitting copies of your VA award letter or by logging on to eBenefits and printing your VA award letter. Veterans are eligible when:

1. Veteran is considered to be totally and permanently disabled due solely to his/her service-connected disabilities, or
2. Veteran is being paid at 100% rate because he/she is unemployable due to service-connected disabilities.

State benefits

Veterans should contact the state office of Veteran's Affairs for more information on available benefits such as license or any tax-related benefits that they may be eligible for (or the surviving dependent of a veteran). Veterans pay reduced yearly taxes on home purchases and in certain states yearly taxes on home purchases! Veterans are exempt from paying state offices. Veteran's Affairs website is: http://www.va.gov/statedva.htm.

Commissary and exchange privileges

Veterans who rated 100% P&T or individual unemployability (IU) get the use of commissaries, exchanges, and morale, welfare and recreation (MWR) retail facilities in person and online. Veterans and service members have unlimited commissary and exchange store privileges on military bases. Other classes of people also qualify, such as un-remarried surviving spouses and dependents of service members who died on active duty, military retirees, recipients of the medal of honor, and veterans whose service-connected disability was related 100% or totally disabling.

You must complete **DD form 1172 – application for uniformed services identification and privilege card.** You can visit the nearest military base to get an ID card to get on base. I remember when I was awarded 90% with TDIU, I went to the VA regional office to request paperwork to get an ID card to get on base. The VA regional office pretended not to know what I was requesting but later denied me assistance in getting the paperwork by saying I must be 100% permanent and total. But knowing the rules and regulations, I went home and logged on to eBenefits and printed my award letter that stated I was total and disabled individual unemployable (TDIU). The next day, I visited the local military base with my VA award letter and received my military ID with no problem! Every time I visited the VA regional office, they gave me hell and the run around by preventing me from getting my benefits before and after I was awarded disabilities by the judge in Washington, DC. It took me 21 years of fighting the VA tooth and nail, holding their feet to the fire, to receive all of my due benefits.

Free parking at airport and cruise terminals

Veterans can park their vehicles for free at the airport and cruise terminals when traveling. Please let the attendant know you have a disabled veteran plate if you're 100 percent and don't have a disabled veteran tag. Don't forget to contact the airport and cruise terminal parking to verify the documentation needed. You can log on to eBenefits to print your award letters to submit. Veterans who are permanent and total with individual unemployability get the same benefits as a veteran with 100% P&T. Each state may require different eligibility.

Defense Finance & Accounting Center

Defense Finance and Accounting (DFAS) is for retired veterans who have been discharged from the military. Contact DFAS if you need help with your military retired pay. You should keep your address and phone number updated once you have retired from the military. The Defense Finance and Accounting website is: **wwwdfas.mil**. The website has a lot of information about military retiree pay issues including MyPay. The commercial number for DFAS for calls outside the United States, Alaska, and Hawaii is 216-522-5955.

DFAS Cleveland
Anthony J. Celebrezze Federal Building
1240 E. Ninth Street
Cleveland, Ohio 44199-2055
Phone: 800-321-1080

VA life insurance

Disabled veterans who separated from service on or after April 25, 1951 are eligible for life insurance, including their survivors. You must **complete VA form 29-4364 - application for service-disabled veterans' insurance**. You may apply for up to $10,000 in life insurance under the Service-Disabled Veterans' Insurance (S-DVI) program. The only requirement is that you must apply within two years from the last date of your award letter from the VA. If you are totally disabled, you may apply for a waiver or premiums and you may be eligible to get additional supplemental insurance coverage of up to $30,000. However, any amount above $10,000, you will have to pay for additional supplemental insurance. You must meet the following requirements:

1. Be under 65 years of age.
2. Be eligible for a waiver of premiums due to total disability
3. Apply for additional insurance within one year from the date of notification of waiver approval on the basic S-DVI policy.

The VA website has complete details and other life insurance programs at www.insurance.va.gov/ or call VA's insurance center at 800-669-8477. You can also mail any information such as your file number, date of birth, social security number, and military records to:

Department of Veteran Affairs
Regional Office and Insurance Center (PH)
P.O. box 7208
Philadelphia, PA 19101
Fax: 888-748-5822

Burial and memorial service

The VA provides burial and memorial services to honor certain deceased veterans. You can order a VA headstone or marker by completing VA form 40-1330 - application for standard government headstone or marker. Submit VA form 40-1330 along with the veteran's discharge papers DD-214. To check on an order destined for a private cemetery, call 1-800-697-6947. Allow 30 days for the application to be received and processed.

Veterans and retired Guard/Reserve are eligible for an inscribed headstone or marker at any cemetery at no cost. Spouses and dependent children are eligible for a headstone only if they are buried in a national or state veterans cemetery. The VA provides the following benefits for deceased veterans:

- VA can honor a veteran by furnishing an inscribed headstone or marker at any cemetery, or a medallion in lieu of a headstone or marker to affix to one that is privately purchased.
- VA can provide a presidential memorial certificate (PMC) for the next of kin and loved ones of a deceased veteran.
- A veteran and his or her dependents can be buried in a VA national cemetery.
- VA can provide an American flag to drape over the casket of a veteran.
- VA can provide a burial allowance to partially reimburse the burial and funeral costs to certain veterans.

Eligibility for burial at Arlington National Cemetery is more restrictive than a private cemetery. Arlington is located across the river from Washington, DC. It is the final resting place for military heroes, presidents, common soldiers, and sailors. You are welcome to contact them for more information:

Superintendent
Arlington National Cemetery
Arlington, Virginia 22211
Phone: 703-607-8000
Website: www.arlington-cemetery.org

Personal Request

I am asking that if you feel you enjoyed this book and feel it has been beneficial to you in learning about The Game Changer: How To Obtain Veterans' Disability, Social Security, And Appeals, please write a POSITIVE REVIEW so that other people might be convinced that they too, can obtain hard earned VA Benefits.

Conclusion

In conclusion, we have reviewed how veterans must take ownership of their claims. Second, veterans must learn how to successfully navigate the VA and social security system for disability benefits by studying the rules and regulations for each disability! Third, we have discussed proper forms and medical records to submit to the VA, your employer, and social security.

Next, veterans must know that independent medical opinion letters come only from private doctors, which is a requirement for every disability in the VA regulation. VA doctors will not write nexus letters or medical opinions for veterans to qualify for disability! We have discussed how to keep your claims from being lost or sitting on the shelf. We have also discussed how to speed up the process of disability claims by seeking treatment from private doctors within 6 to 8 months before retirement or discharge from active duty. Remember to continue seeking treatment from doctors before and after your reserve unit is called to active duty to document medical treatment. This is crucial and in the law to qualify for VA disability! Next, you should start or continue getting medical treatment from doctors within one year of discharge from the military and it must be documented in your military records that you sought treatment while on active duty. You also need proof that you continued to get ongoing treatment. Seeking VA and social security benefits is a process.

Keep in mind, if the VA denied you for a disability, you should still submit VA medical records to social security, which will help build your case for social security! When applying for social security, it is easier if you submit all VA letters and medical records, including from employers, and doctors' letters to social security. Submit medical records to your social security lawyer. You are either disabled or you're not disabled with social security. So submit everything to all agencies.

It took me 21 years to reach my goal of permanent and total status with the VA. This is not a sprint, but a process of faith and determination. By reading and meditating on my book day and night, your dream will come to pass. Keep in mind, you will not win VA decisions every time. There will be setbacks, delays, detours, and disappointments. But you should never give up fighting for your disability benefits. That's why I wrote this book; to give you options and different paths to achieving permanent and total status with the VA and to help you win social security benefits.

Every day God wakes you up, He is giving you another chance to get it right. I don't have it all together. I'm a work in progress! So have faith in God and He will direct your path. You just have to put your faith to work if you want it bad enough. I hope my vision in this book helps someone in their endeavors in pursuit of their VA and social security benefits.

Sharing my knowledge in this book has been a dream come true, high calling, and legacy fulfillment. I hope my book will bless someone! And when you've been blessed, you have a mandate to go and bless someone else in their time of need. That's how you become great in the Kingdom of God by serving one another. My name is Jimmy Cave, and I approve this book!

"**Ask,** and it will be given to you; **seek** and you will **find; knock**, and the **door** will be **opened** to you."- **Matthew 7:7**

VA phone numbers

Bereavement counseling. 1-202-461-6530
Civilian Health and Medical Program (ChampVA) . . . 1-800-733-8387
Caregiver support 1-855-260-3274
Debt management center. 1-800-827-0648
Dept of VA records management records 1-888-533-4558
Dept of VA records management fax. 1-314-679-3732
Education 1-888-442-4551
Federal Recovery Coordination Program 1-877-732-4456
Foreign Medical Program 1-888-820-1756
Headstones and markers 1-800-697-6947
Health care. 1-877-222-8387
Homeless veterans. 1-877-424-3838
Home loans 1-888-827-3702
Life insurance 1-800-669-8477
National cemetery scheduling. 1-800-535-1117
Pension Management Center 1-877-294-6380
Presidential Memorial Certificate Program 1-202-565-4964
Special health issues 1-800-749-8387
Telecommunication Device For The Deaf (TDD) 1-800-829-4833
VA benefits hotline. 1-800-827-1000
VA Combat Call Center 1-877-927-8387
VA Complaint Office 1-855-948-2311
VA complaint about an appeal 1-202-273-7453
VA medication refund 1-866-258-2772
VA fax for an appeal #1 1-202-530-9325
VA fax for an appeal #2 1-202-343-1889
VA status of an appeal 1-800-923-8387
VA Regional Evidence Intake Center. 1-844-531-7818
Veterans crisis hotline 1-800-273-8255
Women veterans 1-877-222-8387

VA web sites

Burial and memorial benefits . . . . www.cem.va.gov
Caregiver support . . . . www.caregiver.va.gov
ChampVA . . . . www.va.gov/hac/forbeneficiaries/forbenefciaries.asp
eBenefits . . . . www.eBenefits.va.gov
Education . . . . .http://www.gibill.va.gov
Environmental exposures . . . . www.publichealth.va.gov/exposures
Health care eligibility . . . . www.va.gov/healthbenefits
Homeless veterans. . . . . www.va.gov/homeless
Home loan guarantee . . . . www.homeloans.va.gov
Life insurance . . . . www.insurance.va.gov
Memorial certificate program. . . . . www.cem.va.gov/pmc.asp
Mental health. . . . . www.mentalhealth.va.gov
My healthevet . . . . www.myhealth.va.gov
National resource directory. . . . . www.nrd.gov
Prosthetics . . . . www.prosthetics.va.gov
Records . . . . www.archieves.gov/st-louis/military-personnel
Returning service member . . . . www.oefoif.va.gov
State Department Of Veterans Affairs. . . . . . www.va.gov/stateedva.htm
Women veterans . . . . www.womenshealth.va.gov
VA vet centers . . . . www.vetcenter.va.gov
VA home page . . . . www.va.gov
VA forms. . . . . www.va.gov/vaform
Vocational rehabilitation and employment. . . . . . . www.VetSuccess.gov
VA homeless program . . . . http://www.va.gov/homeless/index.asp
National Coalition For Homeless Veterans. . . . . . .http://www.nchv.org
The grant and per diem program . . . http://www.va.gov/homeless/gpd.asp
VA medical center facility locator. . . . .
. . . . http://www.2.va.gov/directory/guide/home/asp?isflash=1

About the author

Jimmy Cave
U.S. Retired Veteran

Email: **info@veteransgamechanger.com**

Served 3 years in US Army – Fort Wainwright: Fairbanks, Alaska

Served 10 years in Air National Guard:
- Dobbins Air Reserve Base - Marietta, Georgia
- Dannelly Field - Montgomery, Alabama

Served a tour in Iraq Operation Enduring Freedom:
- Armed Forces Reserves Medal with "M" Device
- Air Force Outstanding Unit Award with Valor Device

Bachelor's degree in Human Resources Management - Faulkner University - Montgomery, Alabama 12/2000

Associate's degree in Human Services - University of Alaska - Fairbanks, Alaska 5/1998

Former Employers: Vet Center, VA Medical Center, Veterans Benefits Administration, Montgomery Job Corp Center

Supporter of Boys & Girls Club Of America
Supporter of Feed The Hungry

CPSIA information can be obtained
at www.ICGtesting.com
Printed in the USA
BVHW052352031021
618070BV00005B/288/J